June /96

Happy Birthday
Andrew.

Love
Don, Lois, Jim & Scott

WINDSURFING

THE CALL OF THE WIND

WINDSURFING
THE CALL OF THE WIND

Text by Shimon-Craig Van Collie
Photography by Darrell Jones

B. Mitchell

A FRIEDMAN GROUP BOOK

Copyright © 1992 by Michael Friedman Publishing Group, Inc.

ISBN 0-7924-5744-7

WINDSURFING
The Call of the Wind
was prepared and produced by
Michael Friedman Publishing Group, Inc.
15 West 26th Street
New York, New York 10010
for SMITHBOOKS LTD.
113 Merton Street
Toronto, Ontario
M4S   1A8

Editor: Suzanne DeRouen
Art Director: Jeff Batzli
Designer: Robert W. Kosturko
Layout: Maria Avitabile
Photography Editor: Christopher C. Bain

Typeset by Classic Type Inc.
Color separations by United South Sea Graphic Art Co.
Printed and bound in Hong Kong by Leefung-Asco Printers Ltd.

windsurfing terminology

When Hoyle Schweitzer and Jim Drake applied for their United States patent in 1968, their board and sail device was simply called a "Wind-Propelled Vehicle." Early monikers for their creation included pet names for individual prototypes, such as Old Yeller, Big Red, and The Door. Once in production, they were called SK-8s (skates) and the Baja boards. In 1969, Bert Salisbury of Seattle came up with the term "windsurfing," which seemed to fit the new sport perfectly. Windsurfer® became, and remains, the registered trademark of the product sold by Schweitzer's corporation, Windsurfing International, Inc.

Had the Windsurfer® been the only board on the world market, the sport's nomenclature might have remained simpler. However, competition sprang up, some of it duly licensed under terms of Schweitzer's patent and some illegally, or from countries in which no patent was ever applied for or granted. Legal battles ensued, and other names for the sport soon appeared, such as boardsailing, sailboarding, free sailing, wind riding, and just plain surfing, in an attempt to avoid problems.

In this text, Windsurfer® refers to the actual one-design board now being sold by Windsurfing International, Inc. Boardsailor denotes one who uses a board and sail of any make or model, as does sailboarder, wind rider, sailor, and any other variation of those terms. The lower case windsurfing identifies the sport in general.

contents

the call

The fog that kissed the eucalyptus trees in San Francisco's Golden Gate Park this summer morning has thinned, evaporated like a lost love. The golden sun has ascended into the cerulean dome, cresting over the Bay's still waters, over the monoliths of downtown and the Victorian flats of the Western Addition. I can sense the city pulsing, with trucks unloading on Market Street; with shoppers bustling in Macy's and Nordstrom; and with bankers and brokers trading on Montgomery Street.

To the east, I can see over the level tops of the Berkeley hills to the rising pyramid of Mount Diablo. Further to the east, the San Joaquin Valley heats up. Its warmed air, redolent with the smell of grapes, peaches, and strawberries, rises in waves over the hardened roadbed of Interstate 5, where four- and eighteen-wheelers race north and south.

San Francisco Bay offers some of the world's most consistent and heavy summertime breezes. Wet suits are required all year round, however, as the water temperature rarely rises above 60 degrees.

The recent Mistral Worlds showcased boardsailors from around the world while San Francisco provided its unique and charming skyline as a backdrop.

Mother Nature spreads long, silky fingers to the west, tugging the invisible curtain of cooler air over the Pacific, seeking to soothe her heated breast.

People like me, some buried in home offices in the Haight-Ashbury area, others in high-rise cubicles along the canyon of California Street, monitor trees, flags, and the wispy puffs of white clouds to the west for signs of wind. Eyes gauge its strength. As green leaves begin to pirouette in the chilly puffs, our hopes rise. When the large American flag atop Nob Hill's Stanford Court Hotel spreads its red, white, and blue wings and flutters noisily in the increasing gusts, heart rates begin to rise. Foggy tendrils grasping the coastal hills create visible signs of stress, including sweaty palms, dilated eyes, and thin beads of sweat on our upper lips.

Around the Bay, we place calls to the Windtalkers, devices that link wind-sensing equipment to a mechanical voice that faithfully records the current conditions:

"Over…the…last…15…minutes…the…wind…has…been…from…the…west…

northwest…at 18 miles (30 km)…per…hour…."

At a certain point, we reach critical mass. The report due tomorrow will just have to wait. The call to a potential client can be made later. Like a militia called to arms, we boardsailors spring into action. Rooftop racks are secured; boards, masts, sails, and wetsuits are loaded up. Silk ties are loosened around the neck as young professionals sprint for the nearest bus connection to their flats in the Marina, where their sedans await, fully loaded and ready for the hunt.

Windsurfing, as those of us who pursue it as a pastime or a vocation have discovered, isn't a sport. It's an obsession.

Few can resist the lure of windsurfing. The sight of board, sail, and rider glissading over the water's surface creates excitement and attracts people. Glenn Taylor, one of the pioneers of the sport, recalls traveling to Europe in the early 1970s and having people jump fully clothed into the sea to ask him what was this thing he was riding. Windsurfing appeals to the human desire to fly, to break free of the constraints of gravity and friction, and to soar over the sea's surface like a bird or some giant, winged fish.

Unlike sailboating, in which the wind's power is harnessed by ropes and wire, the boardsailor forms a living link, a rigging of muscle and bone, that interacts directly with the elements. And unlike surfing, which can take place only where sea and shore meet, the boardsailor can chart his or her own course, be it across the harbor or over the horizon.

Imagination has played a very significant part in windsurfing's phenomenal growth. How could the dreamers who first developed the concept of a freesail rig on a surfboard visualize all that would transpire in less than twenty-five years: that a boardsailor would become the fastest sail-powered watercraft in the world; that aerial aquabatics would produce rolls and spins rivalling the moves of a gymnast; that the sport would become one of the Olympic sailing classes; that adventurers on sailboards would cross most of the world's great oceans and significant straits; that millions of North Americans, Europeans, Asians, and Australians would come to relish this unique endeavor.

But back to the chase. I am among the frenzied mass who have abandoned workaday chores and whose only concern now is to reach a favorite launching spot. I drive over the crest of Pacific Heights, one of the city's tonier districts. Over the roofs of well-painted Victorian houses, I can see the crumbling fortress of Alcatraz, and beyond it the green and gold Angel Island. Between these landmarks and the Golden Gate to the left, the greenish blue waves are flecked with white. My senses quicken, knowing that it's small-sail weather and I will not be disappointed with what I am about to encounter.

The Golden Gate, spanned by its famous orange bridge, funnels the onshore wind and fuels the boardsailor's power requirements.

I plunge down into the Marina, mentally reviewing a list of everything I need: sail, mast, boom, board, wetsuit, harness. Check. I park at the water's edge among a row of roof-racked cars. All about me there are half-rigged sails, masts, and booms on the pavement, the grass, and the seawall that separates land from sea. The wind is not only churning up the Bay, but lifting the sand from the beach and carrying it in a thin, biting stream from left to right. The mighty, hot valley to the east sucks the cool Pacific air and anything else that cannot resist the pull into its belly.

My excitement is tempered only by a slight twinge in my stomach. I will be on the edge out there. The waves and the wind will stretch, twist, and beat on my muscles, tendons, and bones. Unlike tennis or golf, where the playing surface lies passive underfoot, the Bay can hit back. When the tide flows out through the narrow opening under the famous red bridge, it can also carry me out to sea. Those of us who love this sport know its dangers. Testing ourselves against those forces adds a delicious edge to our hobby, whether here on San Francisco Bay, in the crashing blue surf of Maui's Hookipa, or at Western Australia's Lancelin Beach.

I rig up, sail flapping briskly until I can tie it down, stringing its bow tight between mast and boom. I climb into my wetsuit and harness, on the back of which I have a pouch containing a spare universal joint for connecting mast and board in case of a failure at this critical juncture. I also carry extra line, three flares, and a whistle. Luckily up to this date, I have never had personal need for them, although I have used the spare line a few times to tow in other sailors whose equipment failed.

Sail and board rigged, I stand at the water's edge and watch those who are already sailing. As colorful and as free as butterflies, they flit back and forth playing with the wind. As they approach the shore, I can hear the boards chatter as they bounce off waves taken at 25 miles (40 km) an hour or more. Their riders, arms and legs extended, with sails pulled back for maximum thrust, buzz straight toward the beach. At the last second, they tilt the board like a waterskier at full throttle, throwing up a plume of spray. For the experts, a simple flip of the sail and they are off again at full speed. For the less confident, a slight hesitation in the maneuver and they begin to sink as the board slows. For the unprepared, a wind gust picks them up and hurls them like a slingshot into orbit and they crash headlong in a salty shower of foam.

It's time to join them. Holding the sail upright, I jump aboard. A puff whistles through the Gate and tugs the sail from my arms. I hook my harness into the line attached to the boom, which relieves the pressure, and the board rises quickly onto a plane. Before I reach Anita Rock, the large steel and concrete buoy fifty yards (45 m) offshore, I am moving at full speed and steering to avoid incoming traffic.

The ebb tide has begun its twice-daily run, emptying millions of gallons of water through the Golden Gate. Boardsailors love this confluence of wind rushing in and water flowing out, setting up short, steep chop. Water and wind collide, and I bounce from wave to wave, occasionally launching off a short, steep wave face, my board flying like a hooked marlin out of the sea. I move into the aft straps and lean back, pulling the foot of the sail down until it licks the water's surface and creates an efficient foil that pierces the salty air.

The power of the sail surges through my hands, elbows, shoulders, back, and legs. I glance over my left shoulder and watch the Bay race by. Inside I am calm and steady. I can hear the water rush noisily past my feet, spray flying off the back edge of my board.

In the middle of the Bay, the wind pressure drops slightly as I cross into a smooth ribbon of old flood, or reverse, tide. It's time to jibe back. I unhook the harness, press down on the leeward rail with my right foot and guide the board into a 180-degree turn. I release the boom from my right hand and the sail flips effortlessly. I switch hands on the leading edge of the boom and reach out with my left arm to regain power. Visually I check my bearing on Anita Rock, now a mile and a half (2 km) distant, against the sandy shore. I rock back, pumping wind into the sail and lifting the board back onto a plane. I hook in, lean back, and resume my flight.

Perhaps because I am out of earshot of any other human—in twenty-five knots of breeze, the human voice is a weak instrument—I indulge myself in a joyous, maniacal scream. I whoop. I holler. I am free, like the wind, which has swallowed me up, and I release myself to it. My body has atomized, exploded, into a rainbow of colors.

Once or twice, I have been found out in my glee by another boardsailor, who either smiles or responds with a corresponding cry. Here we are, the apex of the evolutionary chain, transformed into boisterous banshees bellowing into the teeth of a gale and loving it. In the eye of the wind, we are holding the tiger by the tail, dancing, on the edge. This is why we windsurf.

One hour stretches into two, then three. As the sun descends, the earth cools and reclines in preparation for sleep, having no more need for the wind. The fog creeps back through the Golden Gate, ready to take up residence for the night. The yellow orb of the sun nestles itself into the cottony down. For those remaining on the water, it's time to return to shore, to derig, to rinse off both equipment and self, and to head back to apartments, homes, and motels. The night permits rest and refueling. Tomorrow, blades and foils will again slice water and air. As the last rays of golden light reflect off the downtown high-rises and the window panes of bay windows on the eastern hills, the fog horns belt out their warnings to mariners.

With visions of speed and spray dancing in our minds, we sleep, contented.

the marriage of SURF and SAIL

Land of surf, sun, and movie stars, California has produced icons, heros, and movements that the rest of the world, willing or not, has followed, from the discovery of gold to the creation of the human potential movement to the birth of personal computers. Creative minds appear to thrive in the Golden State, perhaps encouraged by the sweeping vistas or the balmy air that sweetens the soul.

Amid other 'happenings' of the 1960s, two Southern Californians, Hoyle Schweitzer and Jim Drake, shared a creative spark about merging the merits of sailing and surfing. Their efforts, along with those of others, resulted in the development of a unique hybrid sport that has captured the imagination of people around the world.

The idea of combining a floating board with a sail system had been knocking

Competitors weave their way upwind on racing longboards. They're rewarded with screaming reaches once the weather mark has been turned.

around for more than a few years. In 1941, for example, Hawaii's Albert (Riki) Ebisu put a sloop rig on a 10-foot (3-m) hollow surfboard for the purpose of going fishing for papio in Maui's Kahului Harbor.

Others in various locations around the world also claim to have made similar craft. In 1965, S. Newman Darby printed plans for a square-rigged, 10-foot by 3-foot (3-m by 1-m) door-shaped board on which one could enjoy the sport of "sailboarding." The device's mast simply rested in a hole on top of the centerboard case. The freedom of movement allowed it to pivot, thereby adapting to different wind directions and also changing the board's heading. If the wind blew too hard, Darby advised the craft's pilot to simply throw the kite-shaped sail overboard and paddle.

Darby's invention, which never received a patent, failed to capture the public's imagination. The winds of fortune blew more favorably, however, for Schweitzer and his designing partner, Jim Drake, an aeronautical engineer. The pair devised their own free sail system, the first few versions of which resembled Darby's sailing door. Instead of a rectangular shape, however, the Schweitzer/Drake craft was patterned after the Malibu surfboard typical of the 1950s. The wishbone booms bracketing the triangular sail permitted the skipper to stand on either side, while the centerboard and small skeg on the stern gave the device directional stability.

Opposite page: From a foam blank to a finished product, Larry and Blake McElheny shape, glass, and customize a short board. Below: With foot straps and a willing rider, the final product is ready for a test run. Following pages: The Hook on Hood River serves as an unrestricted docking ground for boards of all shapes and colors.

The key to the sailing board, which went by several monikers, including Big Red, The Door, the Yellow Submarine, and Baja Board (because of Schweitzer's frequent outings south of the border for camping and equipment testing), was the mast-to-deck connection. According to Hoyle Schweitzer, they first tried a rigid attachment to the daggerboard wherein the mast could rotate freely. Tilting it forward and back moved the daggerboard in the opposite direction, a system that soon proved inefficient. The next iteration involved attaching the base of the mast to the board with a short rope so that it was completely free not only to rotate but to move in all directions. Jim Drake, who had thought long and hard about the free-sail system, also tried a sailboat's gooseneck fitting, the device that attaches boom to mast and swings freely in most directions. Eventually, Schweitzer devised and manufactured his own solution. Patented in 1968, the Windsurfer® concept was shared by Schweitzer and Drake until 1973, when the latter sold his portion for $36,000.

Convinced that he could create a market for the new product, Schweitzer quit his job as a computer executive. The family's garage became a factory where Hoyle pressed teakwood into large wishbone booms and built 12-foot (3.6-m) boards of foam and fiberglass. His wife, Diane, sewed the brightly colored sails, while their children Matt and Tara boxed up the boards for delivery.

The unbridled advancement in sail design has hallmarked boardsailing's development, as have the rainbow of colors that are as much fashion as function.

The new invention put the Schweitzers, Jim Drake, and others who gravitated to their circle at the edge of a new frontier. Windsurfing, as the sport came to be known in 1969, not only combined the worlds of sailing and surfing, but the synergy of the union opened up many new possibilities. Using the sailing dinghy as a yardstick against which to measure their forays into the unknown, this band of adventurers explored ways of enjoying their new craft.

Triangular course racing around fixed buoys was an easy step, but for variety they also took their craft into the surf, an environment that a rigidly stayed sailboat does not favor. In 1974, the first "surf-and-sail" contest took place, combining both disciplines. On Saturday, the group would race around the buoys on San Diego's protected Mission Bay. On Sunday, they'd shift to the ocean shore off nearby Tourmaline Street. Contestants would ride the waves and the judges would score their performance from the beach.

While the Windsurfer® resulted from years of serious thought and design, some of the advances and refinements in the sport have come, as they often do, from accidents. By the early 1970s, young Matt Schweitzer had developed into one of the sport's first devotees. He recalls riding his stock Windsurfer®—made from rotationally molded polyethylene plastic (the same durable material that is used to make Frisbees®) filled with polyurethane foam—in the ocean one day and hitting a sand bar. The impact broke his daggerboard in half.

Not wanting to interrupt his sail, Matt headed back out for another ride. He noticed that the board didn't head up into the wind as it usually did. When he jibed back to catch the next wave, he found that at high speed the board didn't 'rail up' or tip over due to water pressure on the daggerboard. He also found it easier to position himself on the wave. Intrigued, Matt began building himself shorter and shorter daggerboards, an idea that soon spread throughout the ranks of other wave riders.

If America was the fountain of innovation, Europe became the engine that drove windsurfing's rise to popular acceptance. Unafraid of immersing themselves in cold water and keen on the idea of a simple, portable sport not unlike snow skiing, Swedish, German, French, and Dutch enthusiasts grabbed ahold of the concept with gusto in the mid-1970s. The first shipment of boards went to Sweden, followed shortly by a "seeding" of a thousand boards to German jet-setters. Windsurfing became the Continental rage.

The Dutch multinational company, Nijverdal TenCate, entered into a licensing agreement with Schweitzer in 1973 to supply the soaring demand. Glenn Taylor, one of the sport's pioneers in the United States, recounts in his seminal book, *Windsurfing: The Complete Guide,* that the TenCate brass donned wetsuits one cold midwinter's day and plunged into an icy Dutch lake to learn how to operate this new equipment to which the corporation was committing millions of dollars.

Matt Schweitzer moved from California to Maui to take advantage of Hookipa's natural charms, like this moving ramp.

Sue Harris demonstrates the merits of a chest harness, which acts like a second set of arms and distributes the load of the sail to the upper torso.

The investment paid off. In the five-year period between 1973 and 1978, about 150,000 boards were bought in Europe from TenCate and other manufacturers. Not all were licensed by Schweitzer, a fact that was to set off years of legal wrangling. Nevertheless, the converts to boardsailing could not be stopped. There was some magic about this sensation of gliding over the water's surface that touched the inner spirit.

Europe was not without its technical contributions as well. Per S. Fjaestad of Sweden, who ordered that initial shipment of Windsurfers® from Schweitzer, designed and built one of the first land simulators. A group of German sailors came up with their own version at the same time. Simulators cut learning time by as much as two-thirds, accelerating the sport's spread in Europe and the rest of the world. The devices let newcomers get the feel of being on the board without going through the windswimming stage of learning.

You won't find the term "windswimming" in any official sailboarding dictionary. I devised the term from my own early contacts with the sport, unaided by the simulator or any official instruction. Thousands of pilgrims all over the world learned the same way, having survived the ignominy and frustration of struggling with the seemingly simple sailboard.

Windsurfing is a sport that few can resist trying. Yet as anyone who has tried it will tell you, fulfillment does not always follow desire. Having been a sailboat racer for most of my life, I figured learning how to get my friend's Windsurfer® up and going one summer afternoon in 1978 would be simple. You just align the board and sail at 90-degree angles, pull up the sail, sheet it in and…SPLASH! Let's try that again…sail up, pull the mast forward, sheet in and… SPLASH! Welcome to windswimming.

The development of teaching techniques and equipment has eliminated prolonged 'windswimming' sessions for beginners. Of course, there are times when being in the water is as alluring as being on it.

Different emotions swept over me for the next two hours. At first I was giddy and slightly embarrassed. Falling into the cool mountain lake felt refreshing, and I balanced my technical failures with the awareness of getting an invigorating workout. Eventually, frustration set in, followed not long after by an anger that approached rage. I swore upon the graves of my ancestors that I would not let a silly toy beat me. As the sun began to set and I noticed that I had drifted almost a mile (1.6 km) from shore, panic began to set in. Finally, I managed to work my way back to the beach, where relief washed over me. I had merely survived, but that was good enough. Like a musician born to play an instrument or a hockey player born to skate, my will to windsurf was stronger than the physics of failure.

My experience was not a solitary one. Thousands of others survived their baptismal sails, or were aided by simulators and a growing rank of boardsailing instructors. Sales of boards continued to grow. By the end of the 1970s, Schweitzer had licensed authorized manufacturers in

Foot straps keep the sailor attached to the board. Nevin Sayre enjoys extended hang time as a result. Multiple foot strap options (opposite page) allow the rider to adjust for different points of sail as well as wind and wave conditions.

Shades of Icarus soaring toward the sun with wings of polyester. Unlike his Greek forebear, this orbiter heads for a gentler splashdown.

Japan, Australia, and Africa. In Europe alone, more than 1.5 million boards of all makes were sold from 1979 to 1984, even with patent battles raging. European manufacturers also advanced board construction techniques, using a hard plastic shell over foam instead of Schweitzer's ding-resistant, but relatively soft, polyethylene.

In the United States, One-Design Windsurfer® races became the most popular outlet of the sport. Sailboarding fleets sprang up, sailing on lakes, reservoirs, bays, and rivers. Weekend regattas became major social gatherings built around one-design racing, freestyle, and slalom competitions.

And of course there were those eager to push the frontiers back even further. In the mid-1970s, a group of mainland boardsailors, including Mike Horgan, Larry Stanley, and Pat Love, relocated to Hawaii. Operating out of a sailboard shop in Kailua on Oahu's North Shore, they started venturing into the blustery trade winds and heavy surf found on the island's windward beaches. The extreme conditions demanded more than the stock Windsurfers® could provide.

Robbie Naish was one member of this pioneering group. He had migrated west in the late 1960s to pursue his passion for surfing and catamaran sailing. Windsurfing's appeal immediately drew him into the fold. He and the others found it very expensive to repair their polyethylene boards, and soon they began making their own boards out of foam and fiberglass, not unlike Schweitzer's original models. To their delightful surprise, they found their new boards were faster than the stock editions. Working with this more malleable medium, they began to experiment with shapes and sizes.

Two other developments resulted in further breakthroughs. The chest harness, a fabric jacket with a hook in the front, attached to the boom, relieved the strain on the arms, and allowed one to sail for hours on end. Footstraps appeared as the Hawaii wave jumpers began to get more and more air time and needed to stay attached to their craft. By screwing rubber straps into the deck for their feet, they could make a firm connection. Like a sailboat's wire-and-rope rigging, the human body became an integral component of this wind-and-water machine.

Not blessed with an overabundance of high wind and waves, Europeans adapted to their environment with round-hulled Open Class boards with sharp V-bows for sailing upwind in light air. Off the wind and in a breeze, these designs required acrobatic skill to keep upright. The soft bilges rolled at the slightest provocation. They also resisted jumping up onto a plane. Nevertheless, they were well suited for Europe's lakes and rivers, and their riders developed a high level of competitive and recreational skill.

Back in Hawaii, boards kept getting shorter and shorter because they were easier to sail in the waves. Mike Waltz, whose family had been one of the inner circle in the development of the Windsurfer® in California, discovered the waves at Hookipa on Maui in 1978. Two years later, his

Many different design approaches to the same problem: how to move through two viscous fluids (air and water) with minimum drag and maximum speed.

friend Mark Paul showed up from Australia with a board just six feet (2 m) long and 32 inches (80 cm) wide. They sailed the "big disc," as Waltz called it, for a couple of days before it blew out of the back of Mike's truck on the way home one evening. Figuring that they could just as easily sail on a real surfboard, Mike went around Maui buying old dinged boards and screwed universal joints onto their decks. They, too, worked, and all of a sudden the gap between surfing and sailing had truly been bridged.

The popularity of the One-Design Windsurfer® faded at the beginning of the 1980s, due in part to a shift in the popular focus from enjoying an afternoon of sailing on the local lake to following the wave sailing exploits of Mike Waltz, Matt Schweitzer, Robbie Naish, and their cronies on Oahu and Maui. The media, both print and video, soaked up images of sailor and board rocketing off wave tops and hanging high against the backdrop of azure seas and cottony trade wind clouds.

Attention then turned to making the sport both easier and more exciting. The short boards, known as sinkers because they couldn't support their rider at a dead stop, were easier to control once you got them on a plane. They were also faster and more exciting.

In many ways, windsurfing became the hotbed of innovation for sail-driven craft in the 1980s. Free from the constraint of arbitrary class rules, designers and builders were limited only by their imaginations and the physics of hydrodynamics and aerodynamics. Hulls sprouted squared-off sterns, rounded sterns, pin tails, and rounded tails. Hull bottoms came out flat, veed, and with single to multiple concavities. Skegs resembled donkey ears, footballs, and airplane wings complete with flaps on the leading edge.

Sails, too, underwent radical transformations. The original triangular snape of the sail gave way to more efficient bird wing configurations, and shortening the booms helped increase the sailor's control over the sail.

In the early 1980s, designers began to attack the soft sail, which had only three short battens in the leech. Its biggest drawback was the tendency to backwind at higher wind speeds. More often than not, that situation resulted in the sailor being slam dunked to windward. Ideas from hang gliders and fixed-wing airplanes began to infiltrate windsurfing. Before he had even learned how to sail a board, Bill Hansen, a pilot and applied physicist, realized that full-length battens running from leech to luff would help. By making the sail more rigid, its airfoil shape could be locked in and held steady over a wider wind range. Using his homemade sails at the Berkeley Marina on San Francisco Bay, Hansen learned to sail his board in a fraction of the time that it was taking others.

This rigid foil approach, also called a rotating asymmetrical foil (RAF), remained incomplete, however. The front end of the battens still floated free of the mast and sometimes tended to poke out in front. Designers attempted to create a device that would both hold the battens firmly against the mast and also allow the sail to rotate freely.

In 1984, a flurry of patent applications resulted from the invention of camber inducers, devices that looked not unlike miniature shuffleboard pushers. The devices held the battens firmly against the mast and "induced" the proper sail shape. In addition, they permitted the sail to move from one side to the other and still hold the airfoil. Instead of a soft sail, boardsailors now had a powerful, semi-rigid wing with which to harness the wind.

Jeff Magnan, a hang glider who has applied fixed-wing concepts to sailboard sails and one of those credited with inventing the camber inducer, says advances in one part of the sport allowed other areas to develop as well. Sails with camber inducers proved significantly faster. With more thrust at their disposal, board designers then created shapes that could attain even higher

The marriage of form and function—Tom Pace broadreaches across one of Aruba's pristine bays with sail, board, and body in perfect trim.

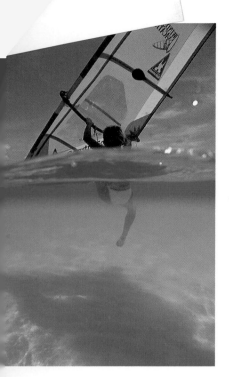

speeds. Off-the-rack boards and sails incorporated these new features, making the adrenaline rush that kicks in around 20 knots accessible to both professional and recreational sailors. "I'm feeling the need for speed" became the boardsailor's refrain.

The public perception of windsurfing as a daring sport, with sinewy acrobats hurtling through space at hair-raising speeds, may have scared away some who wanted to give it a try. In the late 1980s, interest appeared to taper off, and manufacturers began to feel the pinch. The sport's organizers and leaders realized that they had to water the roots to keep the leaves green. In the United States, they began to emphasize entry-level activities, sponsoring learn-to-windsurf promotions and goodwill tours to supplement the more visible racing events.

"I'm constantly being asked if windsurfing takes a great deal of strength," teacher/racer Rhonda Smith-Sanchez told me recently. "My answer is always no, you don't need [strength] to glide across a lake or feel a surge of speed when the wind fills your sails."

In fact, learning to windsurf is now easier than ever. Instructors have acquired a vast reservoir of knowledge since they began giving lessons two decades ago. Using a wide, stable

board with a small sail and light booms and mast, a neophyte can gain a degree of competence with just six hours of lessons. The dry land simulators, which sit on the beach and give the feel for sailing, have been joined by an electronic, computerized version, which presents the novice with any kind of wind and wave conditions desired. Other advances include indoor lessons (with the wind provided by powerful fans), an inflatable collar that can be used like a bicycle's training wheels for stability, and teacher-to-student waterproof radio communication.

Statistics show that beginners can now progress through the learning stages much more rapidly. In the early 1980s, it took almost three years of sailing before the average participant mastered the waterstart. Instead of uphauling the sail while standing on the board, waterstarting allows you to let the wind and sail pull you up to the standing position. A decade later, that skill can be mastered within the first year of windsurfing. Within two years, you can be sailing a short board, a transition that took twice as long ten years ago.

In 1969, windsurfing's co-inventor Jim Drake wrote of the sport that "it could be that there are still many useful maneuvers and techniques of greater difficulty which are as yet undiscovered." How prophetic he was! In the span of two decades, this novel idea has given birth to innumerable innovations and embellishments. The original board and sail that emerged from the early experiments of Pacific Palisades now appear quaint. The original delight and exhilaration that those pioneers experienced, though, remains. Indeed, as shared by those who have come after them, it pushes the sport into new areas of growth.

You can get the feel of the wind on the sail from dry land. Adding water is the tricky part. Opposite page: During a waterstart the sail pulls you up instead of the other way around. Kicking with the back foot assists the process.

CHAPTER THREE

FIVE sports in ONE

Windsurfing's multidimensionality adds to its appeal. For humans of all ages, persuasions, and aptitudes, there is some aspect of board and sail that can fulfill the quest for personal expression, physical workout, or hearty competition. Many sailors enjoy several disciplines, although more often than not they will derive the most pleasure from excelling in one. Following are some views of the different types of boardsailing activities, including very personal views from those who derive intense satisfaction from each. Note, also, that these categories aren't frozen in time. Just as designer Jim Drake never imagined the variations that would result from his simple board and sail, we can only ponder what the future may hold for boardsailing.

Wave sailors seek air time, like giant seabirds rising above the waves. Geert Vanden-Berg gets some altitude at sunset.

wave sailing

As the sport's name implies, windsurfing owes much of its existence to the original, primary board sport, surfing. The original twelve-foot (3.6-m) Windsurfer® board, in fact, was patterned after an enlarged "Malibu" surfboard typical of the 1950s. Riding the surf has always been a part of the sport, starting on the gentle, rolling waves of Malibu and off San Diego's Tourmaline Street.

When the pioneers tackled the big waves of Hawaii in the mid-1970s, maneuverability became important. Boards became shorter for easier turning. Today, surfsailing boards average around eight to nine feet (2.4 to 2.7 m) in length. Those who frequently sail in the same wave and wind configurations often use asymmetrically shaped boards suited for those conditions. The long side is used to carve a wide turn at the bottom of the wave; the short side allows riders to change direction quickly as they come "off the lip" at the top of the wave. Wave-sailing equipment also has to be more durable, since both the rig and the sailor often get immersed in white water. Wave sails are usually rigged with short battens and a soft midsection so the rider can adjust the sail's power quickly by sheeting in and out.

Easily the most photogenic aspect of the sport, wave sailing pits individual and equipment against foaming surf. Waves act as liquid ramps up which the sailor rides, bursting skyward, where she or he hangs like a seagull in the salty afternoon breeze. The more daring sailors roll and flip and loop, endeavoring to land right side up and continue sailing undisturbed to the next wave. Once outside the surf line, sailors jibe and slide down the wave, turning and twisting to steer the board along the viscous mogul, milking the ride until the wave closes out and dissolves into white mush at their feet. Using the force of the wind on the sail, the riders then jibe out and start the cycle over again.

Dean Karnazes learned to windsurf in Australia while down under as an exchange student in 1978. Two years later he worked in a surf shop in San Clemente, California. He had seen pictures of the new breed of wave sailors who were still discovering the sport in Hawaii, but he had never tried it. That didn't stop him from borrowing an 11-foot (3.3-m) wave board that had been brought to the States from Australia and trying it out. Within fifteen minutes he had broken the mast in the pounding surf, but at the same time he discovered a new passion. He now ranks as one of America's best.

Roger Jurians (opposite page) and Paul Coutts (above) use watery moguls as launching pads for their aerial work. Wave sailing offers the most dramatic images of the sport of boardsailing, although other disciplines have their advantages.

All the waves aren't in Hawaii. Florida sailors like Kelly Sullivan (opposite page) here at Delray Beach get their share of half-mast high days, too. Below: Jockeying for position during a course race in Curaçao.

❝There's still a lot of experimentation going on in wave sailing, even though it started back in 1980. I liken it to surfing back in the '50s, when the sport was a novelty and those who participated were all part of a tightly knit group. When I sail the surf these days, it's rare that I don't know most of the people out on the water.

"You're continually paying your dues in wave sailing. Your equipment gets broken when the surf collapses on it, or you'll land on your rig trying to do an aerial loop. It's the most enthralling part of the sport to watch, though, with the jumps and the long sweeping rides.

"A backward loop is like jumping on a trampoline and flipping over backwards while you hold onto the rig and keep your feet in the straps. You get a quick glance at the sky, the shore, and the wave before you land. Doing a forward loop reminds me of riding down a hill on a bicycle and hitting the brakes hard. I make about 80 percent of my front loops, but only about 20 percent of the backward rolls.

"When I'm looking for a spot to sail, I want conditions known as 'side offshore' winds. That means the wind is perpendicular to the direction the waves are traveling, so that as you ride down the face or jump off the tops the breeze is at your side. If the wind is light, I use a big sail and a regular, 8-foot-6-inch (30.6-m) pintail board, which has plenty of flotation and planes easily. In heavier winds, I put up a smaller sail and use a shorter, asymmetrical board, with a long rail on one side and a short one on the other.

"I judge the conditions by how many turns I can make on the face of a wave. At Waddell Creek in Northern California, you might only get one or two. In Baja, you might get as many as fifteen. It's a function of consistency and the direction of the wind.

"My greatest wave sailing days have been in central Baja, with 6-foot (2-m) waves and 25 knots of wind. Part of the magic is finding those secret spots and enjoying those world class conditions with a few of your friends. ❞

freestyle

Part of the challenge of freestyle is making the difficult look easy. Steve Calloway (above) 'lounges' on the rail with his back to the sail. Amara Witchitong of Thailand (opposite page) performs a rail split while sailing the board backwards.

For those days when the wind doesn't even bother to show up, boardsailors have found a way to entertain themselves and others—with freestyle tricks. The wide, relatively stable One-Design Windsurfer® lent itself to this end, providing a steady platform that turns quickly and easily. Add some athletic ability, some courage, and an imaginative mind and it's not hard to see how the extensive catalog of moves, including spins, dips, rail rides, and flips, developed. The sport of freestyling became so hard to ignore, in fact, that most Windsurfer® championships in the 1970s and '80s, as well as some competitions today, include it as part of the overall regatta format.

A wide, flat board that turns easily is best suited for freestyle, as are a simple mast, sail, and boom with short battens. For the beginner, the best conditions are light winds and smooth water. Simple tricks can include using your feet to turn the board in a complete circle, sailing the board backwards, and standing on the back side of the sail while the board continues moving forward. The rite of passage for a freestyler is the rail ride, which was invented by Robbie Naish in 1976 when he was 12 years old. The move involves tipping the board onto its side and standing on the exposed rail.

Katie Griffith has always had an affinity for boards on water, even if in her youth they were skis on snow. She learned to boardsail in Boulder, Colorado, shortly before attending college in Santa Barbara, California, where she raced actively in fleet and collegiate competitions. Freestyle remains one of her favorite pursuits, and in 1990 she toured the country performing tricks to promote the sport.

❝ Back in the early 1980s when I started sailing, we did course racing, slalom, and freestyle in competitions, so I learned all three. The great part about freestyle is that you can practice it anytime. You don't need a lot of wind or waves. You can go out with a group of friends and help each other with your routines. As a performance sport, it pleases the crowd even when you fall in.

"Much of freestyle is getting the mechanics right. It took time to learn tricks, and I had to watch and think about them. Sometimes a new trick would come to me by accident. At other times, I would get extremely frustrated. When I first learned to rail ride, my shins were bloody from trying. It's very rewarding to master a trick, and you have to keep practicing the old ones while you're learning new ones.

"Flexibility is very important. After my daily run, I include several stretches to keep limber, and I finish off with splits to keep myself in practice.

"I still use an old One-Design Windsurfer® with a soft sail, which is lighter than one with full battens. I learned most of my tricks on that board. The booms are long, which makes it easier when you're doing 360-degree spins, because there's more to push against as you start your turn.

"I have two basic routines for competition. If the wind's very light, I do a lot of sail and board tricks, like 360-degree spins, nose and tail sinks, and pirouettes. You're judged by the degree of difficulty, so if you can get the board up on the rail in light air, you get good points. In heavier air, rail rides are easier. Once you do that, you can add splits and rock the board forward and back, which looks great from shore. You can also do flare jibes and water starts.

"A routine lasts three minutes. I start with the easy, graceful routines and save the harder tricks for last. Dismounts count, so many of us have developed signature moves to end the routine. Some people flip through the booms or cartwheel off or do a triple pirouette. I lie down on the board with my feet up in the air holding the boom, then I quickly stand up and jump off the back of the board through the opening between the boom and the sail.

"My most memorable performance was at the Olympic trials in 1984. We were sailing in San Diego, where the wind is always light. I was very nervous. At the time, I had recently moved to California from the mountains, so I was known as the Colorado Kid. I decided to use that in my routine. I put on a cowboy hat and wore a holster and a gun. To start my routine, I took out the cap gun and fired off a round. I chose the William Tell Overture for my music, which starts off slowly and then gets to the section that sounds like galloping horses. I swung my uphaul rope like a lasso and really hammed it up. The routine went over so well I've used it several other times. ❞

Mastering the rail ride (opposite page) marks your transition from a wannabe to a freestylist.

speedsailing

In the ratio of power to weight, you'd be hard pressed to do better than speed-sailor Sharon Thompson (above). The slender shape of a race board (opposite page) offers minimum resistance.

The efficiency of sail, board, and rider has made speedsailing an appealing arena for those who hunger for greater speed. Racing against the clock has been as much a part of the sport as fleet and slalom racing, and as advances in equipment developed, so did the potential for faster and faster runs. Speed trials, where competitors sprint from one end of a straight course to the other anywhere from 100 to 500 meters (110 to 550 yd) long, have become high profile events. In 1986, in fact, boardsailor Pascal Maka of France created a sensation when he became the fastest sailor in the world, faster than any sailboat or other sail-powered craft to precede him. In 1991, another Frenchman, Thiery Bielak boardsailed a record 43.06 knots. In layman's terms, that's like riding down the freeway at just under 50 miles (80 km) per hour on a big skateboard!

Speedsailing requires sailing from Point A to Point B as fast as possible. Compared to a regular sailboat, the sailboard's high power-to-weight ratio lends itself better to such an effort. For best results, speedsailors use short, skinny boards often not much wider than the length of their feet. The sails use more battens than other racing sails to lock in the fastest airfoil shape. Speed trials are set up so that the sailors reach through the course, and the best times result from flat water conditions and lots of wind. Persistence pays off in this discipline: you keep at it until you catch that big puff while you're running the course and it squirts you forward at a higher speed.

Australian Sharon Thompson, a former body builder, track star, and fashion model, became enamored of speed in windsurfing shortly after learning how to sail in the mid-1980s. She

won the first speed event she entered in 1987 and then went to the Canary Islands and established the record for an Australian woman at just under 30 knots. In 1990, she tied for the fastest woman's time in a new speed circuit in the United States managed by windsurfing veteran Ken Winner.

❝ The thrill of going fast has always appealed to me. I had good speed before I had even mastered tacking and jibing. I also had the competitive instinct. Speedsailing was a way into an exciting part of the sport even though I didn't have much experience.

"The key to speedsailing is preparation. You need to have the right equipment and have it ready to go when you need it. Part of knowing what's right is doing your homework for the conditions of each race. On the international circuit, you'll travel with 1,000 pounds (450 kg) of equipment. My quiver was relatively small, with three boards and seven rigs. The top guys might have over fifty board and fin combinations from which to choose.

"A speed course for an international event has a 300-meter (330-yd) preparation course, a 500-meter (550-yd) course, and then 100 meters (110 yd) at the end so you can cross the finish line at full speed without having to worry about jibing or running into anything. The competitors will be about 50 meters (55 yd) apart, each trying to time their run so they're on the course during the maximum windy period.

"You aim to hit the starting line at full speed. During the run, you're constantly adjusting your stance and the sail and board to react to changes in the wind and water. You don't make major changes, but enough to take advantage of a puff, or to make sure you don't slow down too much in a lull.

"Your basic stance is arms extended with your front leg straight and your back leg slightly bent. Point your toes to keep the board flat. At the same time, you're usually worrying about whether or not you're on the right board or if you have the right sail up.

"Wipeouts can be pretty spectacular because you're moving so fast. If your fin stalls out, the board will start to slip sideways and catch the water on the outside rail. It can all happen so fast you'll be in the water before you know what hit you.

"My most spectacular crash was in the Canary Islands. We were all sailing real close to the shore to get the smooth water. I was following someone else and I thought there was enough water where he had gone, but I caught my skeg in the sand. My hang time was so long that I could hear the photographers clicking their shutters. I also had time to hope I didn't hurt myself too much when I landed, but the water is always pretty forgiving. ❞

course racing

With such strong roots in sailing, windsurfing naturally adopted yachting's basic racing concepts. Contestants start by going upwind through an imaginary line between two buoys, sail to a windward mark, turn downwind onto a reach, jibe around a wing mark, and return to the starting area. This triangle is circumnavigated one or more times before sailing through another imaginary line between two markers to complete the race. Boardsailors have added two or more reaching marks to give themselves a giant slalom course where they zigzag downwind before turning upwind for the next windward leg.

A staple of One-Design Windsurfer® sailing, course racing has become an integral part of professional World Cup racing, which also includes wave sailing and slalom. Course racing is used exclusively for the Olympics, and the Olympic boards are one-design, which means the sails, masts, booms, boards, and fins are all identical. Other classes also race one-design, which eliminates inequalities due to equipment. You can buy one board, one mast, one boom, and one sail, and know that everyone else will have the same equipment. You can also race in the open class, which has no restrictions on equipment and allows sailors who are heavy or light to compensate.

The start of a course race in the Bahamas (preceding page) where each competitor seeks the slightest advantage. A standard course board (opposite page) with daggerboard, sliding mast track, and straps for sailing both upwind and reaches.

Trevor Baylis, a former championship sailboat racer, campaigned for Australian 18s in the early 1980s. These monohull yachts, sailed by a crew of three, traveled at over 25 knots under hundreds of feet (meters) of sail and were considered the sport's leading edge of performance. Trevor discovered boardsailing in 1982 and found its simplicity and speed superior to yachting. He took up course racing in 1986. Within two years, he was among the world's best course racers.

❝ Course racing a sailboard reminds me a great deal of the Aussie 18s. Both are very speed oriented and all of your maneuvers are traumatic. If you screw up, you end up in the water.

"What appeals to me about course racing is the intellectual balance of brute force speed and the racing tactics that come into play. When I started course racing, I couldn't match the speed of others around me, so they could wipe me out in practice. But on the course, I found I could beat them.

"Mechanics are very important in course racing. You have to be able to do all the maneuvers without thinking about them. Tacking a board can be a real project, and it becomes much harder when you start questioning your own ability to get around the mast without falling.

"Out on the course, I'm trying to be conscious of both sailing the board fast as well as being aware of the people around me and how I'm going to get past them and where I want to be on the course. When you get both of those going at the same time, it's very exciting.

"Before a race, I'm trying to figure out what the weather's going to do and which side of the course will be favored relative to the wind and the tide. I'm also choosing my equipment. A few years ago, the choices were fairly simple: a 12-foot (3.6-m) course board, two fins, two centerboards, and three or four complete rigs ready to go. Now we have the regular course board as well as the smaller slalom/course boards for windier conditions. Each of them might have three fins and three rigs too.

"Slalom/course boards don't sail as high into the wind, but they can go as much as 50 percent faster than a big course board. You have to figure out how you want to handle that trade-off. You can get a good start more easily with a course board because you can sail higher into the wind and gain an advantage over the short boards. Heaven help you, though, if one of them gets a good start and blasts off, because it'll be gone.

"Success breeds confidence in course racing. When you're fast, you have a sense of assurance as you make decisions about which way to go up the course. You may even make the wrong choice, but you do it with great conviction. In crowded situations, such as the start, your reputation will sometimes push people away from you and open up a nice space in which to sail away from the starting line.

"The great thing about course racing is that you aren't just sailing back and forth all the time. In a way, you're exploring as you sail upwind to one part of the bay and reach over to another. You're always trying to get somewhere in course racing, which is part of the joy of it. ❞

slalom

Bruce Peterson (above), winner of the 1989 Hood River Gorge Pro-Am, accelerates into a jibe at the mark. Slalom racing calls for speed in the straightaways and smoothness in the turns (opposite page).

As in snow skiing, the fundamentals of boardsailing slalom are simple: get from the start to the finish as fast as possible by passing on the outside of several marks strung out along the course. Unlike skiing races, which time each competitor separately, competition on the water is held in heats (eliminating the less-fortunate windsurfer). The top finishers in each heat advance to the next round until a winner emerges. For the benefit of spectators at big meets, like the annual Hood River Gorge Pro-Am in July, heats are run only when the wind is up. For less formal gatherings, no such minimums are required.

For the gung ho, slalom racing offers excitement. If you think of the high adrenaline rush you thrive on when you go for a run, then you can somewhat understand what's going on here. And if course racing is analogous to track's one-mile (1.6-km) run, slalom corresponds to the 100-yard (30-m) dash. In any kind of wind, heats last anywhere from two to six minutes. Contestants try to hit the starting line at full speed. Reaching the first mark in front of the pack often spells the difference between victory and defeat. Jibes are intense, with not only the mechanics of getting board, sail, and body switched from one side to the other, but also avoiding flying booms and careening boards nearby. Slalom combines the power of speedsailing with the demand for error-free execution and split-second timing.

Bruce Peterson, a native Canadian, moved to the Gorge (a section of the Columbia River in Oregon) and began racing slalom in 1983. He won the Gorge Pro-Am in 1989 and ranks among the world's best in both slalom and course racing.

An abundance of wind and a relatively narrow river makes the Hood River Gorge (above) an ideal slalom locale. World champion Bjorn Dunkerbeck of Spain (opposite page) shreds a tight turn in Aruba.

❝ I like power sailing and going fast. When I go funsailing I'm always blasting around and making turns as quickly and as hard as possible, which is what slalom sailing is all about. You have to learn how to trim the board, perfect the jibe, and come out planing with all these people around you.

"I'm most comfortable racing in the Gorge, because I live here. I can pretty much tell how each day's wind is going to develop, and knowing that eases my anxiety.

"The key to doing well is preparation, which takes place long before race day. You've got to tune your boards and rigs, making sure every little part is right so you don't have to run around in a panic at the last minute.

"I have about four or five sails and three or four board/fin combinations, to handle different wind and wave conditions. It would be unusual to have any more than three of each set up on any given day, but they'll be on the beach ready to go. I can run up and grab the right one for the next heat.

"The courses are set slightly differently each day, so you have to go out and sail them before your first heat. You see what the sailing angles are and which end of the starting line is favored. Sailing the course also gives you the chance to warm up. The scene on the beach, with people trying to psych each other out, can be intense. Once I get out on the water, I can relax.

"You can build up a momentum in slalom racing. I was over early in my first heat of the 1988 Pro-Am, which meant I had to go to the loser's ladder. I could still make the finals, but I had to win seven heats in a row to get there. I was mad at myself for that first race, and I was able to use the momentum to sail better. 99

recreational sailing

For all the attention received by the stars of boardsailing's different disciplines, they represent only a tiny fraction of the sport's participants. For every wave jockey sailing off the lip at Hookipa, there are a hundred gliding across the sunny, placid waters of Lake Del Valle, California; for each speed demon aerating the water at Saintes Maries de la Mer in France, there are dozens of Sunday sailors enjoying a warm, hazy afternoon off Cape Cod's Red River Beach; for every World Cup racer tacking off from the beach at Los Barriles on Mexico's Baja Peninsula, there are a flock of pleasure sailors enjoying the salty breeze on Florida's Indian River; for every serious shortboarder at the Squamish Dyke north of Vancouver, there are a fleet of Australians taking the sun and surf at Sydney's Long Reef.

For many recreational sailors, like Jim Dummit of central California's San Luis Obispo, board and sail provides the equilibrium needed to navigate one's way more smoothly through life. He started sailing in the early 1980s and sailboarding became so much a part of his life that he bought a house on Laguna Lake, a small body of water that receives regular doses of seabreeze from the nearby coast. His office, where he works on computer-related projects, is only five minutes away.

The beautiful turquoise waters of Islamorada in the Florida Keys (opposite page) make for a transcendent sail. You can start boardsailing well at a young age, as this preteen (above) demonstrates in Aruba.

Funsailing with your best friend can be just about the most enjoyment you can have outdoors. World-class racer Nathalie Simon enjoys some R&R (riding and ripping) in Aruba (opposite page).

❝I have a wind clause in any work project I undertake: if it blows, I go. I have my windtalker programmed to call me when the wind velocity reaches a certain level. My sails and boards are rigged and ready to go outside my house. I sail for about two hours and then return to the office, shower, and go back to work. If I can get two hours of sailing in a day, I find I can get a full day's work out of just four hours.

"In the summer, my daughters stay with me and they love to go tandem sailing. I put up a small sail and they stand between me and the boom. When we're underway, I fall off the board and they sail on for a hundred yards (90 m) or more by themselves. They love it. I'm also teaching my fiancée to sail. I tie her board to a 500-foot (150-m) line to pull her back when she gets tired.

"I'm building a palapa in my backyard, complete with an entertainment center, wine cellar, Jacuzzi, and sailboard racks. I've got my own sailing resort for me and my friends.

"There's a group of us who are always on the phone in the mornings, figuring out where the wind will be. If there's breeze on the coast, we'll go to Arroya Laguna, near San Simeon and Hearst Castle, which is by far the most accessible wave-sailing spot. I'm an amateur in the surf, so I go beyond the white water where there's a two-mile (3-km) kelp-protected reef to sail around on.

"My motto is: The only things worth doing are fully exciting. I've never windsurfed to the point where it's stopped being invigorating. I've tried doing nothing but sailing, but that wasn't enough. I've also tried living without it and that didn't work at all. I need sailing in my life to keep it balanced. ❞

the
IMMORTALS

Walking down the street in San Francisco or Denver or even New York City, Robbie

Naish wouldn't draw much interest. A few people might recognize the curly blond hair,

the deep-set eyes, and the strong, square shoulders, but he could be mistaken for any

young, active American male who spent a lot of time in the sun.

Shift the scene to Paris or Tokyo or Amsterdam and you've got pandemonium. In

countries where windsurfing has captured the public imagination and millions of

people own or share a board, Robbie Naish comes about as close to a deity as the law

allows. He ranks as Zeus in boardsailing's pantheon, the measure by which all other

sailors have been and continue to be judged.

For Naish, the contrast between his relative anonymity in his native America

No one has done it as well for as long. Robbie Naish, with his unmistakable US 1111, has defined the sport since its inception.

Friendly and unassuming, the Kailua Kid grew up in the boardsailing limelight. His enthusiasm for the sport has survived the hype, and he frequently enjoys a day off in the surf and the air (opposite page).

(except among fellow boardsailors) and his overwhelming celebrity in other countries around the world is just one of many issues with which the young Hawaiian has had to deal.

The lore surrounding Robbie Naish consumes volumes of magazine pages. The son of a ballerina and a surfer, the towheaded youngster inherited his mother's grace and his father's aquatic instincts. When windsurfing came to his hometown of Kailua, on Oahu's North Shore, Robbie blended the sport into his athletic schedule, which also included football, soccer, surfing, catamaran racing, and skateboarding.

In 1976, the shy thirteen-year-old traveled to Berkeley, California, for the Windsurfer® North Americans. Known for its blustery winds, San Francisco Bay toned down for the regatta and the 89-pound (40-kg) Robbie used his lack of weight to advantage. He didn't win, but he placed high enough to earn himself a free ticket to the world championships in the Bahamas the same year. Again, the wind held back. This time, Robbie emerged as the overall winner.

The Bahamas championship had drawn a huge contingent of Europeans. Sailors from the Continent outnumbered North Americans by eight to one, and the European press attended in droves. The emergence of Naish as champion out of a field of over 600 competitors captured their attention, and his face soon began appearing regularly in the boardsailing media.

For the next fifteen years, windsurfing and Robbie Naish became synonymous. In addition to garnering twenty-one world championships, he is credited with inventing the rail ride freestyle move, which involves flipping the board onto its side and sailing on the exposed rail. He became one of the first sailors to go professional in the 1980s, totally dominating the professional World Cup circuit from 1983 to 1987. He still remains one of the world's premier wave riders, a passion he pursues even on his days off in Kailua.

Guy Le Roux, former editor of *Wind Surf* magazine, says that Robbie's greatest gift has been his instincts, comparing him to hockey's Wayne Gretzky or basketball's Larry Bird. A One-Design Windsurfer® racer himself, Le Roux recalls competing against Naish in the 1979 national

Mike Waltz (above) discovered Hookipa one day on a drive around Maui. The determined Phil McGain (opposite page, top) represents Australia's best. Ken Winner (opposite page, bottom) analyzing yet another issue to the benefit of the rest of boardsailing.

championships at Utah's Dry Creek Reservoir. After rounding a mark with the race leaders, Le Roux looked back to see the sixteen-year-old Naish sail to the opposite side of the course where, sure enough, a new breeze brought him into the lead. A meteorological analysis of the mountain winds by Le Roux showed that Naish's move made sense, but when he asked Robbie why he had tacked away from the leaders he replied: "I just felt like it."

Doing what felt good and playing at windsurfing were integral not only to Naish's development, but also to two of his cronies, Matt Schweitzer and Mike Waltz. Their introduction to the sport dates to its inception. Family friends in Southern California, they first learned the new sport in 1969. Matt's parents, Hoyle and Diane, made them a special board with a small sail suited to their diminutive frames. As the boys learned the fine points of windsurfing, their size helped them win many races in Southern California's light breezes. They likewise terrorized the lightweight fleet in regional and world championships, excelling in all the disciplines.

The lure of Hawaii's big waves and strong trade winds captured their hearts, and both relocated to Maui in the late 1970s. Waltz has been credited with discovering Hookipa, the wave sailor's mecca on Maui's north coast, and with leading the movement to shorter and shorter boards. Like Naish, Waltz and Schweitzer excel in wave sailing, and their pictures graced magazine covers and layouts throughout much of the 1980s. Unlike Robbie, however, they turned away from the high-pressure life of the world tour, contenting themselves with emphasizing the fun part of the sport.

A friend of mine says that if boardsailing were the *Starship Enterprise,* the unquestionable candidate for Mr. Spock would be Ken Winner. Tall, dark haired, and usually very reserved, Winner struck a pose in opposition to the Naish/Waltz/Schweitzer beach boy look. He was, however, a formidable competitor in both one-design and open-class racing from the late 1970s to the mid-1980s.

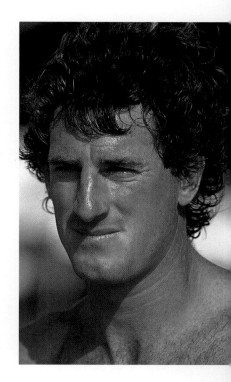

In 1975, Ken bought both a sailboard and a hang glider at the same time and for the same price in his hometown of Annapolis, Maryland. It didn't take long for him to realize that sitting in a sling was much less interesting than holding a sail on a surfboard. He became a talented competitor in all the disciplines, but really made his mark in freestyle. He practiced relentlessly, analyzing every move on the board and creating routines that regularly topped the field. His deductive approach later translated well into board design and other technical aspects of the sport. When boardsailing went pro in the early 1980s, he maintained a top slot, always there, always ready to break through if Naish or anyone else faltered.

While the North Americans wrote their names on many of the trophies in windsurfing's first two decades, sailors from Europe and Australia have always made their presence felt. Australia's Phil McGain, Holland's Stephen van den Berg (the first windsurfer to win a gold medal at the 1984 Olympics in Los Angeles), and Sweden's Anders Bringdal have maintained high performance levels in recent years.

Bjorn Dunkerbeck (below) has matured into a ferocious competitor on the water with speed bursts (opposite page) that amaze his fellow racers.

None has emerged more dominant, however, than young Bjorn Dunkerbeck of the Canary Islands, the heir to Naish's throne as king of the hill. I first saw him in 1986 when he was a tall, gangly teenager on the beach in San Francisco competing in the World Cup tour. He lacked the polish of his older European teammates, but he possessed an inner strength that one sees in great athletes. Strong in wave sailing from practicing at his home in the Canary Islands, he displayed an aptitude for slalom as well. Course racing was the last piece to fit into the puzzle and in 1988 he dethroned Naish for his first of what may be many world championships.

"Nobody dominates the sport like Bjorn," says Bruce Peterson, a Canadian slalom expert who lives in the Hood River Gorge. "It's hard to appreciate the level of speed and control he can maintain and how far he has pushed the limits of the sport. I've seen him blow the start of a slalom race, start 60 yards (54 m) behind everyone else and still win by a whole leg of the course!"

Speedsailing has had its own set of heros, sailors who have totally dedicated themselves to squeezing the last ounce of flight from board and sail. Early attempts at going flat out fast—starting with Hoyle and Matt Schweitzer's pilgrimage to England's famous sailing Speed Weeks in the mid-1970s—showed the potential.

Pascal Maka (above, right) of France has shattered speed records for sail-powered craft. Scott Steele (above) remains one of the world's top tactical course racers after a decade of one-design sailing (opposite page).

In 1983, Hawaii's Fred Haywood became speedsailing's first superstar by breaking the 30-knot barrier. A former college swimmer who had once teamed up with Mark Spitz and Don Schollander in the relays, Haywood radiates a sense of gentle confidence and warmth that belies his expertise and competitiveness.

As speedsailing events generated more attention, other stars emerged. Jimmy Lewis of Maui earned his reputation as a shaper of fast boards and fins and then decided to sail them himself, joining the sport's elite. Frenchman Erik Beale has been near the top spot during the last half of the 1980s.

Leading the speed demons, however, has been another Frenchman, Pascal Maka, looking somewhat like a Shakespearean actor with dark ringlets of hair, a lean face, and a prominent nose. In 1982, he set his first world speed record for a sailboard at 27.82 knots. During the next eight years he led the pack to greater heights, culminating with an astonishing 42.91-knot mark in 1990.

Olympic-class racers rely less on speed and more on finesse and tactics. With its origins in Division II competition that became popular in the early 1980s, Olympic course racing has become a domain unto itself in the windsurfing world. Its leaders have carved out their own identities, such as France's Robert Nagy, New Zealand's gold medalist Bruce Kendall, Canada's Richard Meyerscough, and the United States' Scott Steele and Mike Gebhardt.

As in some other competitive sports, women have had to struggle to gain acceptance in windsurfing. But they have certainly carved their niche, and are fortunate that the sport, in spite of its human-against-nature appearance, requires balance and finesse as much as strength. Women have made their mark in all phases of windsurfing, from course racing's four time national champion Kathy Chapin (1984, 1985, 1987, and 1988) and 1987 World Cup winner Anick Graveline to speedsailing's Patti Whitcomb and Jenna de Rosnay to waveriders Kelby Anno, Dana Dawes, and Angela Cochran.

Few women have been more persistent in the sport than American Rhonda Smith-Sanchez. One of the sport's earliest enthusiasts, she won the women's overall World Windsurfer® Championships from 1978 to 1982. After a brief hiatus, she returned to the competitive wars in the mid-1980s and excelled at slalom racing. She has also taught hundreds of other women how to sail, and remains one of boardsailing's staunchest supporters through her appearances in the media.

For true competitive fire, few boardsailors, male or female, have been able to match France's Nathalie le Lievre. Diminutive in stature and shy in manner, she displayed the heart of a lion by winning four overall World Cup titles in the last half of the 1980s. In 1990, she retired from the professional tour to devote herself to training to win boardsailing's other ultimate achievement, a gold medal in the 1992 Olympics.

Interestingly, the woman who emerged as le Lievre's heiress is the sister of Naish's successor. Britt Dunkerbeck, tall and powerfully built like her older brother Bjorn, burst onto the international scene as a sixteen-year-old speedsailor in 1986, setting the women's record at 33.77 knots. She joined the world tour the following year, emerging as overall champion in 1990.

World champion Rhonda Smith-Sanchez (above) continues to be active as a teacher and competitor. That's her leading the Gorge Pro-Am (right).

While the aforementioned have certainly earned their stars, some of windsurfing's less visible elite also deserve recognition. George Greenough is one. A lifelong surfer, he pioneered the use of shorter boards in the early 1960s and applied the same thinking to windsurfing in the early 1980s. A cinematographer as well, the creative Greenough developed ways to rig cameras on-deck and up the mast to give both participants and landlubbers a first hand feel for the action.

There are others who draw a crowd at the beach when the racers come to town, like board designers Hugues de Turckheim and Larry Tuttle. These creative thinkers have relished the freedom of pursuit in windsurfing. De Turckheim pushed into the realm of developing boards with multiple concavities, or hollows, on the bottom, allowing them to ride more on top of the water than through it. Tuttle, a famous builder of racing dinghies, especially their centerboards and rudders, turned his attention to boards, fins, and foils in the mid-1980s. The products of that effort still provide a benchmark for others to follow.

These are the leaders, then. In truth, these athletes are only mortals whose temperament, ability, aptitude, and sheer determination have found fertile ground in windsurfing, but they are immortal in that their achievements will continue to provide inspiration for aspiring windriders in years to come.

board-sailing MECCAS

Water, water everywhere. The seven major continents are but islands in the global sea, and three-quarters of the planet's surface is fair game for windsurfing. Coastlines, lakes, rivers, bays, creeks, bayous, irrigation ditches, flooded highways, and even indoor pools with large fans supplying the wind at one end offer unlimited opportunities.

Some locations, obviously, have more to offer than others. During windsurfing's first decade, where one sailed wasn't as critical as the fact that one was learning how to master the craft. Having acquired some expertise, boardsailors began to search for new thrills. California, which gave birth to windsurfing, began to yield to Hawaii as the focus of attention. A small group of enthusiasts led by Mike Horgan and Larry Stanley set up camp in Kailua on the north side of Oahu and began deviating from the norm by using foot straps, harnesses, and shorter boards that handled better in the waves.

It's big, it's awesome, it's Maui, and Doug Hunt rises to meet the challenge with a specially shaped boom designed to be easier on the hands and arms.

Charlie Smith (above) goes off the lip at Hookipa where side-shore trade winds make perfect wave sailing conditions. Bjorn Dunkerbeck (opposite page) grabs air with the volcanic backdrop of Maui.

In 1978, One-Design Windsurfer® champion and Southern California native Mike Waltz visited his sister in Oahu and tasted the big waves and steady trade winds of Kailua and Diamond Head. Soon thereafter, he was offered the job as windsurfing instructor at the Sheraton Hotel on Kaanapali Beach in Maui. He "commuted" to work each day on his board and started discovering new spots on the 730-square-mile (1,900-sq-km) island dominated by dormant volcanoes. Besides providing spectacular scenery, the towering craters funneled and accelerated the winds along the island's shores.

As the legend goes, Mike decided to drive around the island one day in 1979 to visit Hana, a secluded and picturesque village on the eastern tip of the island. On the way, he happened to notice a small, semicircular bay on the northern shore with a terrific surf zone and perfect side-shore wind coming from the east. Irresistibly drawn, Mike returned to the site called Hookipa, which means hospitality. He kept returning, enraptured by the consistently outstanding conditions: wave after blue-water-curling-to-white-foam wave from which to jump ever higher and ride from trough to lip. Borrowing money from his friend and former windsurfing student Fred Haywood, Mike quit his job and moved into a house just a few minutes away from his discovery. His only complaint was that there weren't always enough people with whom he could go sailing.

Within a few years, that situation has changed. The word spread. Mike's boyhood chum Matt Schweitzer became an island resident and surf warrior. Photos of Mike and Matt in American

and European sailboard magazines captured the imaginations of others who came to see, to sail, and, in many cases, to stay. For Austria's Mike Eskimo, one of the regulars in the frigid waves at La Torche, France, the lure of the warm waters proved irresistible. For Michigan's Craig Maisonville, the sight of Malte Simmer, Robbie Naish, and Mike Waltz exploring the new dimensions of wave sailing was too hard to resist. Californian Kelby Anno followed her inner voice, the one that told her she was meant to sail and that Maui, a center for spiritual energy, was the place to do it.

Maui became the sport's first major destination, especially after a series of dynamic photographs by Arnaud de Rosnay, one of the sport's first showmen, hit the international magazine stands in 1983. The American publication *Wind Surf* even began dedicating an entire issue to Maui details and highlights every year. Many found it hard to resist the lure of a place where the air and water temperatures rarely drop below 70°F (21°C), or rise above 85°F (29°C), where the summer trade winds blow so steadily that you can shred for as many as forty days in a row, and where the three basic food groups are fresh pineapples, mangoes, and papayas. Like a tropical magnet, Maui attracted the complete range of windsurfers from world-class riders to the wannabes to the vacationer out to enjoy two weeks of sun and fun.

Eventually, Hookipa and its less radical neighboring beaches, Spreckelsville and Kanaha, became overcrowded. Although Maui had it all, including climate, wind, and waves, alternatives began to seem appealing. Sailors in the Pacific Northwest and Canada began to hear about "the Gorge," a section of the Columbia River some 50 miles (80 km) east of Portland, Oregon, where the wind really blew. Unlike Maui, you could drive there (or take a bus or even the train) and pitch a tent on the banks of the river for a day, or a week, or forever, it seemed.

And the wind did blow. Locals began to refer to them as "thermonuclear" breezes, in part due to their intensity and also out of deference to a pair of nearby nuclear power plants. All along the 50 miles (80 km) of river were spots to launch—and to be launched. During the summer months, when the hot desert air of eastern Washington State sucks the cool ocean breeze from the west, the wind exceeds 13 miles (21 km) per hour for more than 400 hours a month. In June, July, and August, the anemometer tops 30 miles (50 km) per hour for over 100 hours a month. Running counter to the westward flowing river, the wind kicks up five-foot (1.5-m) waves that make perfect launching ramps for the aerial gymnasts.

Once again, as tales of the Gorge spread, the outsiders began to arrive. The sleepy hamlet of Hood River, Oregon, became a boomtown of windsurfing shops, board shapers, and sailmakers. Local legends were created, and pet names flourished.

Doug's Beach owed its moniker to Doug Campbell, one of the early devotees. Bozo Beach, on the Washington side, served as a collection point for those sailors who broke down or who were unable to make it back to the Oregon side of the river. Swell City refers to the extra wind and wave height that characterize the section of the Gorge found four miles (6 km) west of Hood River.

When the wind doesn't blow, which is rare, the Oregon/Washington countryside offers fishing, river rafting, skiing, and a nearby metropolis in Portland. River touring on a sailboard is another option, giving sailors a chance to explore their Bali Hai.

The Gorge became boardsailing's mecca. The sport's luminaries, like Ken Winner and Rhonda Smith-Sanchez, bought into the local real estate market. A new epicenter had been founded, and the discovery once again brought the hordes. The term "boardhead" began to surface as a description of one who lives to sail and sails to live, and the Gorge was the place to fulfill that destiny.

"We heard there was wind on the Hood River." There was, indeed, and there continues to be, enough to satisfy the throngs that come to find out for themselves.

The Gorge (below) offers a shredder's paradise where the wind blows year-round. The action is so intense that safety becomes an issue for some (opposite page) who don helmets, facemasks, and gloves for protection. Pages 84–85: A lone windsurfer is inspired by the beauty and serenity of this landscape in Portugal.

Yet, being in the northern latitudes, the Gorge still had its drawbacks. A wet suit is necessary most of the year, and the winter can get downright chilly, even for the hard-core windsurfers. Where could one find the perfect mixture of heavy winds and mild temperatures that would make the truly ideal windsurfing spot?

In 1988, a Corpus Christi, Texas, dentist by the name of Dr. Charles Allen helped inaugurate the U.S. Open Championships at his favorite sailing spot. Located on the southeastern shore of the Lone Star State, Corpus Christi offers the most wind of any American city that has both warm air and water. The hundreds who attended the Open, where winds never fell below 18 knots, came away with yet another location to add to their list. Names like Oleander and Bird Island Basin entered the boardsailor's lexicon as part of Corpus Christi's bountiful offerings.

Conscious of what windsurfing had done for the economy of Hood River, the local politicians and business gurus jumped on the bandwagon, too. They cleaned up the beaches and made attractive offers to boardsailing equipment suppliers. Local sailors also came up with the notion of a Boardsailing Hall of Fame, which will hopefully do for Corpus Christi what baseball has done for Cooperstown.

The formula became quite easy: find wind. Find warm water. Go there. Sail a lot. Tell your friends. They all come, too. Pretty soon you've got a new windsurfing center.

Jay Valentine "discovered" the southeastern coast of Baja California, Mexico, one night while watching a home movie at a dinner party in San Francisco. It wasn't what the characters on screen were doing that intrigued Jay, who caught the windsurfing bug in 1978, but the great number of white-capped waves in the background. He ventured south for a scheduled two-week vacation and ended up spending ninety days out of ninety-six experiencing full planing conditions. The Sea of Cortez, where Hemingway had once roamed with his buddy Doc Ricketts collecting sea specimens, soon became prized for its consistent winter winds. Sailors riding their *chico barcas*—little boats—beat a path to its beaches.

This Portuguese coastal village offers yet another backdrop for this pair of sailors.

Americans weren't the only ones exploring new vistas. Australians ventured out from the early One-Design Windsurfer® centers like Sydney to find bountiful offerings to the north and west. Repulse Bay, inside the Great Barrier Reef on the continent's northeast coast, features 30-knot trade winds, cold beer, and September Fun Week. On the opposite side of the continent, exploring sailors from around the world have enjoyed 1,000 miles (1,600 km) of undeveloped coastline both north and south of Perth. The famous Fremantle Doctor is a cooling wind that soothes the heated coast during Australia's summer months from November to March. The desert town of Lancelin has become a favorite destination, with a reef-protected bay and wave sailing outside for the more adventurous.

Remote Margaret River, two hours south of Perth, has developed cult status among globe-girdling sailors. Entrance and exit to the prime sailing spot require navigating through a four-foot (1.2-m) widebreach in a barnacled rock reef. Only one person can ride each wave, which may peak out at two and a half masts high, putting it on a par with the legendary surf of Oahu's North Shore. The treacherous reef has been known to eat rigs without remorse.

Entering the last decade of the century, it seemed like there were few places you couldn't sail a board. On a layover in Guam, I spent a hot spring morning enjoying a cool sail in a deserted lagoon to leeward of a high rocky cliff. A local legend recalled that centuries earlier, a pair of doomed lovers had tied their hair together and jumped from the heights to their deaths.

Have wind, will travel. From Canada's Squamish Spit (just north of Vancouver) to Cape Town's Bloubergstrand to Italy's Lake Garda to Hong Kong's Stanley Beach and to Japan's Omazeaki, windsurfing is now an international language.

My friend Suzanne Suwanda recently discovered Aruba, the small island off the northwestern coast of Venezuela, where the trade winds average over 20 knots in the spring and over 30 knots in the summer, all day and all night. Hearing her description of the protected reef, flat-water sailing at Fisherman's Huts, and the big waves off the south end of the island created that familiar tug of windsurfing desire in me. I recalled sailing on my honeymoon off the northern shore of Antigua, also in the Caribbean, where the coral heads grow like giant mushrooms under the turquoise blue waves.

Warm water isn't a prerequisite for a boardsailing mecca, except for those sailors who refuse to even consider wearing a wet suit. Colder waters have their own appeal. American Ted Huang, one of the world's best Olympic course racers, lists Gotland, an island off the east coast of Sweden, as one of his favorite havens. Standing like a sentinel in the Baltic Sea with Russia to the west and Germany to the south, Gotland features the tenth-century walled city of Visby. Hundreds of Swedes enjoy their boardsailing each summer on Gotland, with its jagged coastline and the rocky cliffs mixed with windmills and chapels.

Less than a mile (1.6 km) from my front door is another cold water bay, with a spectacular shoreline and, for much of the year, enough wind to make me and hundreds of others quite happy. I'm referring to San Francisco Bay. We may not have the waves of Maui or the nuclear breezes of the Gorge, but it's harder to find a greater variety of conditions in a 50-mile (80-km) radius anywhere else in the world.

Windsurfing on San Francisco Bay dates back to the early 1970s, when Glenn Taylor and Ted McKown started selling One-Design Windsurfers.® Glenn, a computer programmer from the South Bay, became a one-man promotional fireball, running races, giving lessons, and inventing teaching aids. Ted was one of Glenn's first customers, and later opened his own shop just north of the Golden Gate Bridge in Sausalito.

A ship of the desert meets boards of the sea in Morocco. Both offer transport to a more desirable state of mind.

Both Glenn and Ted dropped out of the sailboard scene when one-design sailing lost its momentum in the 1980s. Many of the sailors who learned from them, however, carried on into the era of short boards and full-battened sails. I include myself among them.

While those of us who live near the Bay may travel to other locales to get a taste of something different, we all know that back home we have something special. Those hungry for an easy sail or a freestyle practice session can drive inland to Livermore's Lake Del Valle, a peaceful oasis carved out of a California hill. For a little more challenge, there is Alameda's Crown Beach, one of the few warm beaches on the Bay. For a more aggressive day on the Bay, drive up the freeway for an afternoon off the Berkeley Marina, or over the bridge to San Francisco's Crissy Field. With the Golden Gate Bridge on your left, Alcatraz on your right, and the city's unmistakable silhouette in the background, it's hard not to get caught up in the grandeur of the place. And don't forget the 25 knots of westerly pushing you over two-foot (60-cm) chop just to make the picture complete.

But there's more. For a speed blast, head north to the Sacramento River Delta, a mini-version of the Gorge. The hot valley to the east draws the cool coastal air in at a ferocious speed, and the flat river water provides a smooth runway. For a more leisurely pace, drive over the coastal hills to sail the surf at Stinson Beach or Waddell Creek down near Santa Cruz.

Those of us who call San Francisco Bay home appreciate its variety of windsurfing locales, but we also realize there's literally a world of windsurfing out there waiting to be explored.

the adventurers

On the morning of May 24, 1986, I stood on the sandy shores of Drake's Beach and peered out at the western horizon. A thin layer of hazy fog covered the juncture of sea and sky. Thirty miles (50 km) to the southeast stood the Golden Gate Bridge, entrance to San Francisco Bay. On this day, however, my thoughts stretched to the west to a small crop of craggy rocks known as the Farallon Islands. Rigged and ready to go with a 12-foot (3.6-m) cruising board and an old Windsurfer® sail, both of which I had borrowed, I was about to attempt the first crossing out to the islands and back, a round trip of 44 miles (70 km).

Standing with me on the beach were my fiancée, my mother and brother, who had come 3,000 miles (5,000 km) to be there for the big event, and a dozen other

Boardsailing across an ocean is like riding a bicycle across the desert: pretty crazy and achingly irresistible for those with incurable wanderlust and an exaggerated sense of adventure.

Solace from shore-bound concerns is one of the sea's great gifts, purchased by those willing to tread upon its waters.

friends who had helped put together the Farallon Challenge, as the event was known. Also present were a four-man support crew, complete with a high-speed powerboat that would accompany me on the way. One of the crew, a doctor, had agreed to help only if I gave him the right to tell me to get out of the water if I became too tired or delirious. I granted him that privilege.

Some would say I was already out of my head for attempting such a stunt. The waters of the Gulf of the Farallones are reputed to be among the roughest in the world, and the area around the islands serves as a breeding ground for great white sharks.

Windsurfing opened new vistas for explorers, wanderers, adventurers, and thrill seekers. The lure of heading out to sea with only a thin sliver of a board on which to ride and a piece of sail-cloth for power captured many adventurous imaginations. Like all great athletic achievements, windsurfing across great expanses of water pits a person against both nature and himself and provides an unequaled opportunity to explore and discover the true self with all the accoutrements of civilization stripped away. By the end of the sport's first decade, such challenges were becoming popular.

In February 1979, Ken Winner covered 100 breezy miles (160 km) of Florida coastline in less than seven hours. Six months later, France's Baron Arnaud De Rosnay sailed his board through the Iron Curtain, covering the 85 miles (136 km) from Alaska to Siberia in eight hours. Before the year was out, another Frenchman, Frederic Beauchene, tackled and mastered the

North Carolina's Cape Hatteras (above) provides this sailor with launching power.

sailor's ultimate Everest by rounding Cape Horn on his sailboard. Less than a year later, Anne Gardner and Jack Wood (on separate boards) sailed 70 miles (112 km) across Lake Titicaca on the border of Peru and Bolivia, the world's highest stretch of water.

Success bred confidence, and soon bigger feats were attempted. In 1980, De Rosnay organized an expedition to sail 2,000 miles (3,200 km) from the Marquesas to Hawaii. Originally intending to go with a 40-foot (12-m) sailing sloop as a support boat, he abandoned the idea when he discovered the yacht couldn't keep up with his planing board.

The French Navy, which had helped with the preparations, then tried to prevent De Rosnay from pursuing the venture, but the determined sailor, who claimed baronial lineage, would not be stopped. He had trained himself to sail during the day and derig at sunset, using his mast as a steadying cross beam with floats on the ends and an inflatable collar around the board as a sleeping shelter. During the night, he would fly a kite, which would pull him along his course. For navigation, he learned an ancient technique of crossing two sticks and focusing on a certain star.

Under the cover of night, De Rosnay decided to go alone. After battling sunburn, sharks, and a lack of food and water, he washed ashore thirteen days later in the Tuamotus, 750 miles (1,200 km) from his launching site. The outrageous feat and the baron's flamboyant public persona created a furor not only in the boardsailing world, but politically as well. The French government and press railed against his reckless ways. Prudent seamen of all nations questioned his mental health. Yet certain sailors got a faraway look in their eyes on hearing of his exploits—at last, they had a bona fide hero to emulate.

I counted myself among that group. Living in San Francisco and working in Marin County to the north, I drove nearly every day across the Golden Gate Bridge. Whenever the wind blew I saw to the east the horde of colorful sails tracking across the Bay's mouth. If the weather was also clear, as it can be on those quintessentially California days, I could turn my head and see the triangular outline of the Farallones on the horizon.

On one such day, in the fall of 1985, the thought dawned on me that I should windsurf to the Farallones. I had sailed around them a few times in a boat, and I had fished for salmon off the island's craggy coast, but the notion of sailing a board to the edge of the earth, to the farthest distance that I could see, and back, represented a challenge I found difficult to resist.

After work that day I went to visit Ted McKown, a friend of mine who owned one of the first windsurfing shops in Northern California, and told him of my plan. He smiled politely at first, but when the impact of what I had said sunk in, he was shocked. "You're going to what!!??"

My boardsailing skill level at that time was barely past the beginner level. Ted shook his head in disbelief. Yet somewhere behind his initial reaction, I could sense a small glow of

Opposite page: This bird's-eye view of a sailor and his board reveals the beauty of the sport combined with the natural beauty of the environment. Below: Shark's-eye view of a water-start. Does this look like a meal to you? Only if you've got a prehistoric brain and a ravenous hunger.

Formation sailing in Aruba, where the wind averages more than 20 knots for much of the year, day and night.

agreement, a tiny flicker of support. I asked if he would help me out, and he agreed.

As I was to discover, long-distance windsurfing adventures are as much about being supported as they are about hooking into the boom with your harness for hours on end. Logistically, a distance crossing, whether it lasts one day or three weeks, requires tremendous attention to detail. You must attend to eating, drinking, resting, sail changes, navigation, medical contingencies, and myriad other elements. Overlooking what may seem like a minor concern can turn into a potentially major disaster.

Take, for example, Christian Marty, the French airline pilot who became the first to cross the Atlantic without leaving his board in 1981–82. Sponsored by a magazine, a radio station, and a board manufacturer, Marty planned to sail from French West Africa to Martinique in the West Indies, a 3,500-mile (5,600-km) trip. Accompanying him were twelve friends on a 70-foot (21-m) sailing ketch. After sailing eight hours each day, he would pack up his sail, like a clerk heading home from the office, and turn it over to the mother ship. In return, he received an inflatable ring that surrounded his board, and inside of which he slept for the night.

Rudder problems on the ketch after five days forced the expedition to return to port for repairs. The delay caused Marty to readjust his plan. He cut the trip short by 1,000 miles (1,600 km) to land in French Guyana. After thirty-seven and a half days, he reached his goal.

The lack of a simple piece of rope, however, could have resulted in a very different end to Marty's adventure. One night while sleeping, he capsized, an event that happens not infrequently

in the open ocean. Trying to retrieve a sleeping bag that was floating away, Marty lost contact with his board, which started drifting away faster than he could swim. Not realizing anything was amiss, the support crew were surprised to hear him yelling from the dark water a few hundred yards (meters) away from his board, which had righted itself. They picked up the sailor and returned him to the board. From then on, Marty tethered himself to his craft, aware that he had narrowly escaped death.

The ending of De Rosnay's endeavor is less fortuitous. His Pacific adventure was followed by a 1982 crossing of the English Channel in record time, an aborted attempt to sail the 1,900 miles (3,040 km) of the Caribbean island chain in 1983 (he only completed a third of the trip), and trips from Morocco to Spain across the Straits of Gibraltar, from Miami to Cuba, and from Japan to Russia in 1984.

The legend of De Rosnay grew with his marriage to the beautiful blonde Jenna Severson, who tutored at the baron's hand and became a world-class racer and speedsailor in her own right. They were the sport's First Couple, hooked in and planing fast through the global reach of life.

At a certain point in a long-distance sail, you reach the realization that you are a part of the sea and at its mercy.

The poet Carl Sandberg said that "One of the greatest necessities in America is to discover creative solitude." This sailor finds some in the Florida Keys.

According to his friend, journalist Pietro Porcella, De Rosnay had become the victim of his own stardom. His increasingly risky crossings were beginning to scare even him. On the night before what was to be his last great feat, sailing from mainland China to Taiwan (two countries officially at war), he telephoned his wife and expressed fear at the outcome. With neither official sanction nor escort, he set sail on November 24, 1984, and has never been seen since. Many boardsailors around the globe hoped that he would resurface after being released by a military patrol, or be found on a remote stretch of coastline where he had landed when his equipment failed. Eventually, though, many began to believe that he had been transformed from windsurfing's preeminent ambassador into shark bait.

Would the same fate befall me? As I uphauled my sail that May morning two years later, the nervousness in my stomach testified to my curiosity. Mine was not a political voyage, nor was I seeking world fame. Local fame, perhaps. Mostly, I wanted to prove to myself that I could blaze a trail, to go where no person equipped with only a sail and a board had gone before, and not fail when tested to the limit.

The voyage provided ample quantities of limit testing, even if the outer edges of my boundaries were not what I expected. Hoping for a strong sea breeze that would blow parallel to the Northern California coastline and rocket me out and back on a beam reach, I sailed into a fog bank instead. Wind follows the path of least resistance; accordingly, it rose above the moisture-laden fog. That left me with barely enough zephyrs to make my way westward. Without the counterbalancing force of the wind on the sail, I found it difficult to stay upright, falling ungracefully into the sea at least every half hour. As soon as I did, the theme music from the movie *Jaws* started playing loudly in my head as I hastily scrambled back onto the relative safety of the board.

After six hours on the starboard tack, during most of which I could barely see a few hundred yards (meters) in any direction, I spotted white surf crashing on a rocky shore 25 yards (23 m) ahead. I made it!

My original intention had been to round the island and return, but in the fog that would have been too dangerous, not to mention time consuming. It was already four o'clock. Only four hours of sunlight remained. After consulting with my support crew, I decided to simply turn around and head back.

The human body has a remarkable ability to adjust to extreme stress. Holding the booms in the starboard tack position for six hours had stretched the muscles and tendons of my torso and arms asymmetrically. When I tacked the board and tried to sail on port tack, my body could barely manage it. I lost my balance and fell into the water. I struggled back up on the board and tried again with the same result. The question now became whether or not I could even hold the rig for the return trip.

My feat pales in comparison with that of another adventurer, France's Stephen Peyron. In 1984 he windsurfed for seventy hours nonstop, covering 315 miles (500 km) in the process. In 1986, he and his friend Alain Pichavant rode a tandem board across the Atlantic. A year later, Peyron repeated the feat alone on a 24-foot (7-m), 250-pound (112-kg) board with enough room in the hull for him to crawl into when he was ready for a much needed rest.

Peyron's feat capped the cycle of boardsailing feats that had started seven years earlier. With sponsorship from a boardsailing manufacturer and a major food company, as well as extensive media coverage in North America and Europe, he brought windsurfing to the attention of the world in a way no one, not even De Rosnay, had done before.

Compared to his voyage, my trip to the Farallones was a walk in the park. At one point, Peyron was so exhausted that he fell asleep while changing his wet suit and didn't reawaken until

Surfing at night (opposite page) isn't for the faint of heart or the unprepared. With a moon or shorelights to guide you, though, it can be a thrill.

eighteen hours had passed. During that period, the hatch protecting the inside of the hull was open and, had he capsized, the hull would have filled with water and sunk the vessel.

The physical toll was as extreme as the mental strain. Peyron revealed that all his joints were brutalized by the sail, and he vowed not to try another such trip again.

Although my trip to the Farallones was less demanding, there were moments on the way back from the islands when I had to struggle with my inner voices. My arms and lower back ached from holding up the rig for hours on end. I was constantly thirsty from sweating in my wet suit. We still could barely see a few hundred yards (meters) in any direction and dusk was beginning to settle.

Fortunately, the wind began to pick up in the early evening. Finally, I was able to hook my harness into the line coming off the boom, and the board jumped up onto a plane. My long-awaited glory ride had finally arrived.

Unfortunately, my exhilaration was soon dampened. As we broke free of the coastal fog's grasp, I realized that the shore looming ahead of us was far north of our intended landing spot. Between me and the soft, sandy shore at Stinson Beach lay the treacherous Duxbury Reef, a shipkiller for the past three centuries.

I was approaching exhaustion, but now I had to jibe downwind in 20 knots with a big sail to get around the southern tip of the reef. I blew nearly every turn, but persevered until I could see the blinking light marking the end of the rocky shoals to the left of my course. I sailed past it, glancing over only once to see 10-foot (3-m) high surf crashing thunderously into white foam. As the golden sun reflected off the verdant hills above me, I rode the ground swells to shore. Cheers greeted my arrival.

No sooner had I stepped off my board for the first time in ten hours than the sun slipped below the horizon for the night. A cold beer and a hot meal awaited me and I devoured them with the ravenous hunger of the sailor home from the sea.

When asked why he sailed solo across the Atlantic, Stephen Peyron said he did it to discover himself. I shared his sentiment. I was certainly not the most qualified windsurfer to make the trip; others had more experience and better equipment. I had that adventurer's urge, however, and the desire to push myself. Windsurfing allowed me to act on those desires, and provided me with an experience for which I am very grateful.

There were two particular lessons that I learned from my trip. For one, in windsurfing as in life, events don't always turn out the way you imagine them, despite planning. My vision of the ultimate shred across the blue Pacific failed to materialize. The actual sail was long and arduous and my success depended more on perseverance than skill.

The second and more inspiring truth that I learned was the meaning of a quote from the novelist Goethe that I discovered shortly after I decided to make the trip. It, too, applies to a broader context, but for those of us who enjoy this sport so avidly, it can be used to further our goals no matter what they may be: "Whatever you can do, or dream you can, begin it. Boldness has genius, power and magic in it."

Perhaps no windsurfing voyage has more dramatic appeal, however, than the one undertaken by seventeen-year-old Lester Moreno Perez, in the spring of 1990. Perez lived in the Cuban seaside town of Veradero, where he had taught himself how to windsurf years earlier. Attending high school in the evenings, he kept his days free to teach European and Canadian tourists how to boardsail and spent his free time practicing, sometimes as much as eight hours at a time out in the Straits of Florida.

For Lester Moreno Perez, what lay beyond the horizon was America and relatives with whom he could live, free from the restrictions of Castro's Cuba. The youngster hatched a plan for

a daring escape. He enlisted a few friends and some helpful strangers, including a German tourist who gave him a racing-course board, with which to make his attempt.

With a combination of Hemingway bravery and De Rosnay daring, Moreno Perez waited until dark on the evening of March 1, 1990. Creeping along the beach, he rigged his 18-square-yard (15-sq-m) sail and slid into the sea, eluding detection by guards on an offshore observation tower. By studying the wind patterns, he had calculated that the easterly breeze would hold most of the night, making the 90-mile (144-km) crossing to the Florida Keys a bouncy beam reach. Hooked into his harness, he flew across the waves, even jumping off the tops into the night like a flying fish. Around him he saw dark silhouettes, shapes he hoped were dolphins but realized at dawn were sharks.

Ten hours later, his boom broke. By holding the pieces together, he was able to make slight progress, and was picked up by a Bahamian-registered freighter 30 miles (50 km) short of the Keys. Soon after, he was transferred to a United States Coast Guard ship. Within a month he was living with his great-aunt and great-uncle in Hialeah, Florida, enjoying his new home and sailing for pleasure off Miami Beach.

you're a REAL board- sailor when....

You're a real boardsailor when you start scheduling your life around the wind. You find yourself listening with more than casual interest to the hourly weather and buoy update. You become an expert at analyzing forecasted temperature differences between the coast and inland. The greater the spread, the more wind will blow that afternoon. You become an amateur meteorologist. Your coworkers and friends begin to wonder why you rub your hands with glee when storm clouds form on the horizon and the prediction is for rain and gale force winds.

You're a real boardsailor when you get a message that "Dr. Marina" or "Gale Storm" called. That's the code word you and your sailing buddies have worked out for letting each other know that the wind's up and they'll meet you at the beach ASAP. You're

By any standards, Cort Larned, a world-class racer, teacher, and promoter of the sport, is a real board-sailor, from the top of his surf-wet head to the bottom of his full-length wet suit.

able to look a business associate, even your boss, straight in the eye without any trace of guilt and tell them you can't meet at two o'clock P.M. because you have an important meeting to attend. You're also willing to forfeit a promotion if it means you have to work afternoons no matter how bad a business move it might be.

You're a real boardsailor when you shake hands and strangers recoil, inquiring as to why you have so many calluses. You also have calluses on the tops of your feet from being in the straps all the time.

You're a real boardsailor when your pulse races at the sight of white caps on the water and two red triangular flags over the harbormaster's office signifying gale force winds. While fishermen and those who sail boats run for cover in those conditions, you can't wait to get rigged up and out on the water.

You're a real boardsailor when you divert all your disposable income to sails, boards, and other equipment. You dream about how to best complete your quiver of sails and whether you need a new short board. You go to the sailboard shop with the sole purpose of buying a harness line and end up exceeding your credit limit with a new wet suit, a surf sail, and anything else that catches your eye. At the outer extreme, you forego lunches for a month to help pay for a new racing sail.

John Geyer (opposite page) takes a break from the action in Costa Rica. Sloppy Joe's Bar (above) in Key West, where sailors land-jibe after a day on the water.

Ken Rudolfsky hams it up on a Maui beach before he sets out for adventure.

You're a real boardsailor when your conversation begins to feature words like "radical" and "go for it." You describe a change of direction as a "land jibe." You begin to look at your kid's skateboard and wonder if you could mount your universal on it and sail it around the parking lot. You wear a T-shirt that says, "Life's a reach and then you jibe."

You're a real boardsailor when you buy sails in matching colors so your significant other (or your parents) is never able to figure out how many you really have. He or she probably won't know the fine points between a 4.5 and 5.0 square meter camber-induced racing sail, anyway, and you've got sail bags stashed in different parts of the house as a precaution against being found out.

You're a real boardsailor when you always wear your big, black, waterproof watch with the compass rose on the outer dial and the black rubber watchband. When you do take it off, which is only for a medical emergency or at the insistence of a higher authority, its outline is neatly marked by pale flesh surrounded by tan skin.

You're a real boardsailor when you wake up and even though your arms are sore from too much sailing the day before, you can't wait to get out there again. You discover that your hands seem permanently glued in a one-and-a-quarter-inch (3-cm) curl, which is approximately the diameter of your favorite boom.

You're a real boardsailor when you've escaped the jaws of death at least once out on the water and lived to tell about it. Your boom breaks in the middle of the bay just before dusk and you spend the next half hour frantically paddling into shore. You're enjoying a screaming reach and happen to glance through the window in the sail to see a ferry boat about to run you down. You get caught out in a surprise 50-knot gale with a 6.0 sail up and can only sail a board length at a time before you get your face planted. Then you lose one of your contact lenses and have to be picked up by a passing motorboat.

You're a real boardsailor when, although you know you should always sail with a friend, you find yourself out on the water alone, totally immersed in the moment. It could be late on a summer evening or in the middle of a workday when you bagged your job and went out to practice your jibes. You sit down on your board and float with the tide, at peace with yourself and the world around you. You understand what the seagulls enjoy about living on the water. You understand the meaning of satori. You are one with the moment.

You're a real boardsailor when you have so many T-shirts that you don't have to do laundry once during the sailing season. Every time you go to a windsurfing event, part of the entry fee

Nevin Sayre went to the Aruba High Winds Pro-Am and, among other things, he got yet another T-shirt. If you don't wear them again, you can put them on the wall for decoration.

Ian Boyd (below, left) and Mark Angulo (below, right) take a break at Hookipa. The pair have made their mark in wave sailing, where each has pushed the outer limits of 'rad.'

includes an undershirt with the date, location, and other colorful illustrations. In a pinch, you even get so bold as to wear one under a white dress shirt. When you take off your jacket, people can see the outline of a boardsailor exploding off your chest.

You're a real boardsailor when you start watching old *Gilligan's Island* reruns just to see if it's whitecapping off the deserted island. You find yourself scoping out the wind and water conditions shown in movies in the hopes that you'll discover a new mecca.

You're a real boardsailor when the equipment on top of your car is worth more than the car itself. The stack of boards, sails, and masts on your roof rack prevents you from getting into your garage. You begin to ask your friends if they have any extra storage space. You're also afraid that your seats will get wet if you hose off your car because the salt water that drips down from your gear has rusted the roof. When you go looking for a new vehicle, your main criterion is whether or not you can fit all your gear inside.

You're a real boardsailor when you're sitting in class and the professor's lecture becomes less and less audible as the leaves on the tree outside the window start to rustle more and more in the breeze. When the wind reaches planing velocity, you ask your study partner if you can borrow some notes later and head for the nearest beach.

You're a real boardsailor when you start wondering if the next city on your travel schedule has wind during the time of year you're going to be there.

You're a real boardsailor when you make a fool of yourself trying to explain what's so great about windsurfing to a total stranger by extending your arms and dropping into the hooked-in position, face forward, making a chatter-chatter sound.

You're a real boardsailor when you get caught unaware by a monster puff that nearly rips your arms out of your sockets, pulls you into a face plant so violently that you're flipped upside down and land spread eagle on the mast so hard you could have broken your back. After splashdown, you check to make sure nothing's broken, and then you let out a shout of joy.

You're a real board-sailor when the equipment on top of your car is worth more than the car itself. Following page: Another day ends at Aruba's Westpoint Lighthouse.

You're a real boardsailor when your car has enough sand in it to be declared a national park. Ditto for your garage, bathroom, and bed. The latter may in fact remind you of sleeping on the beach. You own two wet suits, neither one of which ever gets completely dry, and the first piece of clothing you put on in the morning is your swimsuit. No need to change when you head out for a sail.

You're a real boardsailor when you've broken equipment through excessive use. On the last leg of a heavy air race, you crack your centerboard in half coming off a wave just 20 yards (18 m) short of the finish line. Planing over a reef, you catch your skeg on a coral head and rip it out of the board. You've been pumping your way onto the face of a wave and the mast cracks where the boom is attached.

You're a real boardsailor when you've had at least one perfect sail. It could have been on a lake one sunny afternoon when you executed every tack and jibe without falling in. You may have found yourself flying across a blue water channel in total balance, just skimming along the top of the waves. It may have been the day you and your friends discovered a totally isolated beach with 6-foot (1.8-m) waves and 25 knots of side shore breeze where you just sailed your hearts out and spent the night sleeping on the beach to do it again the next day.

You're a real boardsailor when you rig up your sail and stick the foot of the mast into the sand to see how it looks in the prevailing breeze. After checking one side, you "tack" by walking around to the other side and testing again. You then point the head of the sail into the wind and dig the tip into the sand so it won't fly away in the next strong puff.

You're a real boardsailor when you learn to judge wind velocity by the height of the sand blowing on the beach. Ankle high is 25 to 30 knots. Knee high is 35 to 50 knots. When it's shoulder high, it's time to head for home and wait out this blow!

When you're in balance, you can even do it with no hands (below), as this sailor demonstrates. Following pages: Eagle Beach in Aruba, a windsurfer's heaven, is the sight of this regatta.

getting BACK to your X in the SAND

Although the title of this book says it's about windsurfing, it's really about emotions. Any sport, really, is about feelings, because if what we do isn't fun or exciting or soothing, we wouldn't do it. Windsurfing fits all three of those categories, and several others as well. For those who've discovered its thrills and beauty, sailing on a surfboard can fulfill many needs: the desire for competition, the ecstasy of going fast, the joy of riding the waves, the adventure of exploring new territory, and the solace of being at one with nature.

Here are the stories of a couple of boardsailors whose profiles you won't see in magazines, but who represent, for me, the human side of the sport.

I have a friend named Mike Monahan. We met in the 1970s when we both raced sailboats on San Francisco Bay. In 1973, he attended a regatta for International 14

A boardsailor's fantasy come true: Maui Meyer explodes off a wave in crystal clear waters with a background of fleecy trade wind clouds.

Powered by trade winds from the Pacific, Robbie Naish handles a roller near his home in Kailua, on the eastern shore of Oahu.

dinghies at Association Island in upstate New York. The World Windsurfer® Championships were being held there at the same time. Mike recognized one of the windsurfers from the Bay Area and asked if he could try out a board. In seven knots of wind and flat water, Mike sailed it out, turned around, sailed back, and said the sport would never catch on. Compared to the high performance dinghies Mike was sailing, the Windsurfer® just didn't cut it.

Ten years later, Mike borrowed another board from a local friend for his second sail. This time he ventured out onto San Francisco Bay, where there were more waves and more wind. With a chest harness, footstraps, and a board that was 20 pounds (9 kg) lighter than the Windsurfer,® Mike began to see the sport's possibilities. He bought his own board and spent two months learning to master it. A year later, he moved to Lanikai on Oahu's east coast near Kailua to fulfil his dream of living on the beach and riding his bicycle to work. He also bought a used short board for $80 and began windsurfing off the beach outside his cottage.

For the serious recreational sailor, Lanikai has much to offer. Kailua Bay's azure-blue water stretches out three quarters of a mile (1 km) over a sandy bottom to a series of coral reefs. The protected inner bay features flat water for beginners. When the easterly trade winds kick in, speed sailors can get their thrills there, too.

Beyond a five-foot (1.5-m) coral mass called Flat Island, mast-high waves break on the outer reefs. The normal trade winds make the breeze side onshore. Mike learned how to weave his way to the right in between waves and then veer left at the last second to get the breeze under the sail while rising off the face of the moving mogul. He learned how to go higher and higher,

reaching up to 30 feet (9 m) above the surface of the sea where he would hang like a giant sea bird surveying the earth below. And he learned where to position himself on the reef to catch the rollers in succession, sometimes jumping sixteen waves in a row until he was laughing out loud from the rapture of being blessed with such a life on this planet.

A board and sail sit idle on the beach at Fortventura in the Canary Islands.

Mike arranged his life so that he went to work early in the morning and got off in time to spend the whole afternoon sailing. Riding home on his bike, he could see wind-bearing squalls darkening the horizon, and his anticipation rose. His sail and board always stayed rigged; ready to go at a moment's notice. He started keeping a record of how often he made it out on the water. In order to make a mark on his calendar, he had to plane for at least an hour that day. Over the years, he's averaged 100 days a year when he could make that mark.

Adding extra excitement to Mike's sailing are the days when his neighbor, the legendary Robbie Naish, comes out to play in the surf. More often than not, Mike simply stares in awe as the sport's king frolics in and above the waves. Last winter, he followed Robbie out through the surf. Off the 9-foot (2-m) faces, Robbie first performed a barrel role, followed by an aerial loop. The five-time World Cup champion topped it off by jibing on the face of the wave without switching position on the board. Naish ended up on the wrong side of the sail, surfing down the wave in perfect control. So stunned was he by the move, Mike didn't notice the wave that clobbered him face on. He disappeared into the white foam as Robbie sailed serenely past.

Recently, Mike's job changed. His work schedule keeps him busy until 4 o'clock P.M., which hinders his sailing. When he needs a fix, though, he goes out at night. He navigates using the street lights near his house. Years of sailing at the same spot have embedded the memory of how to thread through the coral heads. Once outside, he blasts along in 18 to 25 knots of wind, sailing into a night as dark as the inside of a closet with the door closed. It reminds him of a race he once sailed across the Pacific on a 55-foot (16-m) sailboat, roaring down the dark tunnel of night with the spray flying. When the tropical moon lights up the sky, he can see the fish and the coral reefs as he skims over the dappled sea.

Guy Le Roux, Sr. also moved west to take up a new life in the early 1980s. Unlike Mike, who is now entering mid-life, Guy had already raised his family and put in his time behind a corporate desk in New York City. At the age of fifty-three, divorced, and looking for a new lease on life, he moved to California. There his son, Guy Jr., taught him how to sail a board, a turn of events that greatly amused him since he had taught the youngster how to sail a boat decades earlier.

The sea and sailing had always been a part of Guy Sr.'s life. He grew up on the north coast of Brittany in France sailing model boats and converted workboats. During the New York man-in-the-gray-flannel-suit years, he always had a boat in which he and his family cruised and sailed Long Island Sound. Those recreational outlets weren't sufficient, however, to compensate for the psychic price he paid toiling in the steel and glass behemoths of Manhattan. Well read, erudite, and uneasy with an overly structured life, he was glad to leave the East Coast behind.

Windsurfing provided the outlet for which Guy Sr. searched. Free from the workaday world, he explored the waters of San Francisco Bay from Coyote Point to Bodega Bay and the San Joaquin River Delta. Eventually, though, he became a regular at Larkspur Landing, a small stretch of sand and rock in Marin County just a shout from San Quentin state prison. On the northern edge of the Bay, Larkspur features a variety of conditions from easy going on up. When the coastal fog settles over the Golden Gate a few miles to the south, the wind rises above the moisture laden air and returns to Earth on this sunny inlet with powered-up gusts that challenge the experts.

Although ardent in his practice of the sport, Guy Le Roux, Sr. never reached the expert stage. He was content to sail on his large board and big sail, powered up in 16 knots of breeze. A good sailor by his peer's standards, Guy's age and an expanding waistline nevertheless kept him from admittance into the shredder's domain.

Retired and able to spend his time as he wished, he would drive down to the beach in the late morning and sail before the westerlies really started to howl. If there was no wind, he'd hang out at the beach. He became a fixture in the Larkspur scene, a friendly face, a partner who would lend you a spare part or who might ask to borrow one himself. He kept an eye out for people, noticing who had been trying to uphaul for a long time and might need some assistance in getting back to shore.

Making it back to the beach—returning to the X in the sand where you left your keys—is as much a part of windsurfing as the white-knuckle ride or the sun's reflection off the waves. Those of us who sail surfboards have all had moments when we wondered if we were going to make it, if we would see our friends and family again. Danger, whether real or imagined, is always present.

Mike Monahan recalls his moment of truth back in 1986. Launched off a wave, he suddenly found himself separated from his board. The universal joint connecting the mast to the deck broke, leaving Mike holding the rig as he descended into the surf. The next wave picked up his board and carried it toward the beach two and a half miles (4 km) distant. The friends with whom he had been sailing tried to find Mike, but in the large swells only his head was visible, and then only for short periods of time as he bobbed up and down making it impossible to zero in on him. As they crisscrossed to windward looking for him, Mike screamed to catch their attention, but the wind carried away his shouts.

Mike decided he'd have to swim for it. Not wanting to abandon his rig, he hooked it with his feet and started backstroking. When he got tired, he switched to side stroke. To the west, the sky reddened and the sun set. Three hundred yards (270 m) from the beach, a boardsailor came within hailing distance. Mike gave him his rig to tow in and swam the rest of the way himself. On the darkened beach, the members of the local fire department gathered around his board, wondering where its owner might be.

On June 13, 1990, sixty-four-year-old Guy Le Roux, Sr. went looking for wind. Not finding any at Larkspur Landing, he drove north a few miles to China Camp, an old fishing village on the beach that now serves as a state park. Guy sat in his van, listening to music until the leaves began their twirling dance. A few of his friends showed up, and they all started getting ready.

One of the other sailors noticed the older man was having trouble tightening his downhaul, so he went over to help. Guy shoved off in the puffy, 8- to 18-knot breeze and soon fell off his board. He waterstarted and fell again. This time he uphauled, but within a few minutes he was back in the water waving his arms. One of his friends onshore yelled at a passing sailboat to go over and see what was wrong. By the time he got there, Guy was in bad shape. The sailor pulled him aboard and brought him to the beach. CPR brought Guy briefly back to life twice and then an ambulance took him to the hospital.

"The last sound he heard," says Guy Jr., "was the gentle lapping of water on the bottom of a hull."

Guy Le Roux, Sr. didn't make it back to his X in the sand. Shortly after his passing, however, the city of Larkspur approved the installation of a memorial bench at his favorite beach. Guy had often complained that there was no comfortable place to sit while waiting for the wind at Larkspur Landing.

Now there is.

Guy's son says that windsurfing gave his father a renewed enjoyment of life, that the activity and the friendships and the belonging yielded the best years of his life. The same can be said for thousands of others like Mike and myself. We have found in the sport the marriage of excitement and beauty along with the connection of human and nature in an elemental dance. When the waves pound their rhythm on the shore and the wind blows its magic flute, our feet jump and our arms ache to be in its embrace once again.

Following pages: Jan Boersma goes it alone off the island of Curaçao.

epilogue

It's spring, and the chill of winter is melting rapidly. The tangy salt air of the bay fills my nostrils as a reminder that there is sailing to be done. I head for the garage, where my board has sat patiently during the dark months. I unwrap my sail, a brilliantly hued wing ready to once again take flight. The fever is back.

Ultimately, words fail to convey the magic of windsurfing. The sensation of gliding across the water at sunset cannot be found between the covers of any book. The feeling of your heart leaping in your chest as you jump onto your first plane of the day can never be captured in words. Nor can the excitement of gliding down the face of a wave, freefalling in space with the roar of the surf in your ears. Accounts of thrills and adventures can never substitute for the real thing.

This book can serve two purposes, however: first, it can stand as a testament to windsurfing. In twenty short years, the sport has grown from a novelty into one of the fastest growing recreational pursuits in the world, complete with heroes, legends, and organizations dedicated to its growth and development.

Secondly…I hope this book conveys the enjoyment that you can derive from participating in windsurfing yourself. There is no other experience quite like the first time the wind fills the sail and tugs at your arms. You surge forward, venturing ahead into a new world of excitement and enjoyment.

May the wind be always at your back.

appendix I: windsurfing organizations by country

canada

Windsurfing Canada
Canadian Yachting Association
1600 James Naismith Drive
Gloucester, ON K1B 5N4
Phone: 613-948-5687   Fax: 618-748-5688

united states

American Windsurfing Industries
Association (AWIA)
99 East Blithedale Avenue
Mill Valley, CA 94941
800-333-2242 or 415-383-9378

U.S. Windsurfing Association
P.O. Box 978
Hood River, OR 97031

britain and europe

Royal Yachting Association
RYA House, Romsey Road
Eastleigh, Hampshire SO5 4YA
United Kingdom
Phone: 44 703-629962
Fax: 44-703-629924

Professional Boardsailors Association
No. 1 Barn Cottages, Albany Park
Colnbrook, Slough SL3 0HS
United Kingdom
Phone: 44-753-683484
Fax: 44-753-683507

World Boardsailor's Association
Fruhlingstrasse 5, 8200 Rosenheim
Germany
Phone: 49-8031-16035
Fax: 49-8031-33724

australia

Windsurfing Academy
14 Etna Place
Refnyne, WA 6000
Australia

appendix II: windsurfing organizations by specialty

course racing

International Funboard Class Association
163 West Lane
Hayling Island
Hampshire PO 11 OJW
United Kingdom
Phone: 44-705-463595
Fax: 44-34-227732

Lechner (Olympic) Class and Course
Racing
Rudolf Steiner, President
International Board Sailing Association
P.O. Box 6809
CH-3001 Bern
Switzerland
Phone: 41-65-452111   Fax: 41-65-452111

one-design racing

Mistral IMCO One Design
Grindelstrasse 11
8303 Bassendorf
Switzerland
Phone: 41-1-8368922   Fax: 41-1-8364942

Ted Schweitzer
International Windsurfer Class Association
2030 East Gladwick Street
Dominquez Hills, CA 90220
USA
Phone: 213-608-1651

World Boardsailing Association
Fruhlingstrasse 5
8200 Rosenheim
Germany

U.S. Yacht Racing Union
Box 209, Goat Island Marina
Newport, RI 02840
Phone: 401-849-5200   Fax: 401-849-5208

speedsailing

International Yacht Racing Union
World Sailing Speed Record Council
c/o John Reed
Royal Yachting Association
RYA House
Romsey Road
Eastleigh
Hampshire SO5 4YA
United Kingdom
Phone: 44-703-629962
Fax: 44-703-629924

wave sailing

59-397 Ke Nui Road
Haleiwa, Hawaii 96712
USA
Phone: 808-638-7642   Fax: same

appendix III: periodicals

australia

Free Sail Magazine
Box 746, Darlinghurst NSW 2010
Phone 02-331-5006   Fax: 02-360-5367

Sailboard Extra
118A Windsor Street
Paddington NSW 2021
Phone 02-32-1145
or
Suite 6, 11 Beach Street
Port Melbourne 3207
Phone: 03-646-6788   Fax: 03-646-7162

canada

Windsport Magazine
2409 Marine Drive
Oakville, Ontario L6L 1C6
Phone: 416-827-5462   Fax: 416-827-0728

united states

Wind Surfing Magazine
World Publications, Inc.
330 West Canton Avenue
P.O. Box 2456
Winter Park, FL 32790
Phone: 407-628-4802   Fax: 407-628-7061

Southeast Boardsailor
1882 Pineapple Avenue
Melbourne, FL 32935
Phone: 407-254-3117   Fax: 407-242-0904

New England Sailboard Journal
40 South Street
P.O. Box 468
Marblehead, MA 01945-0468
Phone: 619-639-2838   Fax: 617-639-2830

West Coast Boardsailor
94760 South Bank Road
Pistol River, OR 97444
Phone: 503-247-4153   Fax: 503-247-7556

Northwest Sailboard/Wind Surf California
P.O. Box 918
Hood River, OR 97031
Phone: 503-386-7440   Fax: 503-386-7480

britain and europe

Boards Magazine
196 Eastern Esplanade
Essex, England SS1 3AB
Phone: 44-702-582245
Fax: 44-702-588434

Windsurf Magazine
Ocean Publications
The Coach House
Medcroft Road
Tackley, Oxon
England
Phone: 44-869-83677   Fax: 44-869-83733

Planche Magazine
107, rue du Pointdujour
92100 Boulogne
Billancourt, France
Fax: 33-1-49-10-30-41

Wind Magazine
8–10, rue Pierre-Brossolette
92300 Levallois-Perret
France
Fax: 33-1-90-87-92-80

selected bibliography

Taylor, Glenn. *Windsurfing: The Complete Guide.* San Francisco: McGraw-Hill Book Company, 1980.

Fox, Frank. *A Beginner's Guide To Zen And The Art Of Windsurfing.* Berkeley: Amberco Press, 1988.

Coonrad, Jordan, and Elaine de Man. *Wind Warriors* (calendar). Berkeley: Zephyr Press, 1991.

Evans, Jeremy. *The Complete Guide To Windsurfing.* New York: Facts On File Publications.

Jones, Roger. *Windsurfing: Basic And Funboard Techniques.* San Francisco: Harper & Row Publishers, 1985.

Grubb, Jake. *The Sailboard Book.* New York: W.W. Norton & Company, Inc., 1984.

Jones, Roger, and Ken Winner. *Windsurfing with Ken Winner.* New York: Harper & Row Publishers, 1980.

index